M000107323

a concise guide to

Adult Faith Formation

I'd like to put this book into the hands of every parish leader in today's Church. Chapter 4 alone, "God as Teacher," is worth the price of this book. In it, Parent extols intimacy with Christ as the core work of all formation. He turns this vision into reality with doable and realistic planning suggestions for parish programs.

Bill Huebsch
Website Leader for PastoralPlanning.com
Author of *Dreams and Visions: Pastoral Planning for Lifelong Faith Formation*

This is not a book that should be on every adult formation directors' shelf. It should constantly be in their hands, their minds, their hearts. It is practical, perceptive, pertinent, persuasive, and powerful.

Janet Schaeffler, O.P.
Associate Director for Adult Faith Formation
Archdiocese of Detroit

Anyone familiar with adult faith formation will be able to take away new insights from the wisdom and tested pastoral practice reflected in this book. Anyone new to the field will find much on which to build a parish adult faith formation effort.

Dr. Michael Steier, DMin
Associate Director
Secretariat of Evangelization and Catechesis
United States Conference of Catholic Bishops

Neil Parent orchestrates a symphony of practical wisdom and resources to support the emerging adult faith formation leader in both parish and diocese. He elaborates on the historical factors which influenced the adult faith formation movement within the Church, sharing his personal experiences and offering practical guidelines to move one's parish or diocese forward with sensible clues for success.

Sr. Angela Ann Zukowski, M.H.S.H., DMin
Director of the Institute for Pastoral Initiatives
University of Dayton

Confronting and comforting, Catholic and ecumenical, missteps and miracles. Neil Parent does it all. This book puts flesh on the goal of comprehensive lifelong adult faith formation.

Leland D. Nagel
Executive Director
National Conference for Catechetical Leadership

THE CONCISE GUIDE SERIES

a concise guide to

Adult Faith Formation

Neil A. Parent

Kevin E. McKenna, Series Editor

ave maria press AMP notre dame, indiana

THE CONCISE GUIDE SERIES

The Concise Guide series, edited by Kevin E. McKenna, tackles questions of central importance for contemporary Catholicism. Each book in the series carefully outlines the issues, references the necessary documents, and sketches answers to pressing pastoral questions.

Excerpt from the English translation of the *Rite of Christian Initiation of Adults* © 1985, International Committee on English in the Liturgy, Inc. All rights reserved. Used with permission.

Excerpts from the National Directory for Catechesis, © 2005, and the General Directory for Catechesis, © 1998, United States Conference of Catholic Bishops. All rights reserved. Used with permission.

© 2009 by Ave Maria Press, Inc.

All rights reserved. No part of this book may be used or reproduced in any manner whatsoever, except in the case of reprints in the context of reviews, without written permission from Ave Maria Press®, Inc., P.O. Box 428, Notre Dame, IN 46556.

Founded in 1865, Ave Maria Press is a ministry of the Indiana Province of Holy Cross.

www.avemariapress.com

ISBN-10 1-59471-208-5   ISBN-13 978-1-59471-208-1

Cover design by Andy Wagoner.

Text design by Katherine Robinson Coleman.

Printed and bound in the United States of America.

Library of Congress Cataloging-in-Publication Data
Parent, Neil A.
 A concise guide to adult faith formation / Neil A. Parent.
 p. cm.
 Includes bibliographical references.
 ISBN-13: 978-1-59471-208-1 (pbk.)
 ISBN-10: 1-59471-208-5 (pbk.)
 1. Spiritual formation--Catholic Church. 2. Christian education of adults. I. Title.
BX2350.3.P36 2009
 268'.434--dc22

                                2009016835

To my wife Lynn
and to our daughters
Elena, Denise, and Diana
who have taught me more about adult faith
than they will ever know.

Contents

Preface

When Ave Maria Press invited me to write *A Concise Guide to Adult Faith Formation*, I was pleased and honored. At the same time, I began to worry about what I could possibly say that had not already been said, much of it by people far more gifted than I. For example, among the current literature available is Jane Regan's *Toward an Adult Church*, which lays out a compelling vision for a new educational paradigm focused on adults. *Nurturing Adult Faith: A Manual for Parish Leaders*, published by the National Conference for Catechetical Leadership (NCCL), is a treasure trove of solid, practical advice. And RCL Benziger, in partnership with NCCL, has published an adult faith formation module in its *Echoes of Faith Plus* series that provides excellent video and print resources for small group learning.

There are, moreover, the official catechetical documents that have been issued in the recent past, such as the *General Directory for Catechesis* and the *National Directory for Catechesis*. These present authoritative principles on adult faith formation to guide our efforts in this all-important ministry. In addition, the U.S. Bishops' pastoral letter on adult faith formation, *Our Hearts Were Burning Within Us*, identifies the action steps that need to be taken to move the entire enterprise forward in U.S. dioceses and parishes.

I decided eventually on a twofold approach. First, I would address areas where I thought more could or needed to be said. Second, I would address these topics with stories from my own experience as an adult faith formation leader. I especially thought I could help the reader by mining my own failures and successes. I wanted the reader not only to learn from my mistakes but also to realize that becoming a good adult faith formation leader involves both risk-taking and failure. The important thing is not that we always get it right, but that we always try to improve.

In terms of what needs to be said, I am convinced that not enough has been written about adult learners as modern spiritual sojourners. We cannot facilitate adults' growth in the faith if we do not understand what influences their spiritual choices. I also felt that independent learning and God as teacher warranted more attention. Since the advent of the World Wide Web, the learning paradigm has dramatically shifted in favor of greater reliance on independent learning. For this reason, I argue for more self-directed learning in adult faith formation and offer suggestions as to how to go about it.

As for God as teacher, I am convinced that we do not do enough to help adults attend more to the voice of God as their inner teacher. We tend to view the catechetical process almost exclusively in terms of what we do as pastors and catechetical leaders. But as both Augustine and Aquinas have counseled us, God is our primary teacher of the faith, and we need to listen to God's voice.

In this book, I propose five ways to attend to God as teacher. I do not mean to suggest that these are the primary or the best ways for us to learn from God. Liturgy, scripture reading (especially through *Lectio Divina*), spiritual counseling, spiritual reading, and a host of other methods are all aimed at our listening to God's voice. My main focus, rather, is on helping us recognize how modern life often strips away our ability to quiet down and allow ourselves to be taught by God. If we can help adults do this, we have already greatly aided their faith formation process.

The three other topics in the book: parish as a learning community, the adult learner, and program planning have all been written on extensively. Even so, one cannot write a book on adult faith formation without in some way addressing these critical areas. My approach, therefore, was to address them in a way that attempts to engender new insights based upon my own experiences.

Every writer's fear is that so many people have already written on his or her topic that they don't think they have anything more to say. I certainly felt that. But I also remembered the classic advice given in such situations: "Only *you* can write from *your* perspective." I hope my perspectives on adult faith formation prove to be of some value to the reader.

Finally, I wish to acknowledge those individuals who played a special role either in my adult education development or in this book's preparation.

My interest in adult education sparked during my seminary years with the Paulist Fathers. Charles McCarthy, then a Paulist priest, invited me to assist him with an adult discussion group he was leading in Bowie, Maryland. That experience was foundational in my development as an adult educator, especially in terms of small group processes.

Msgr. Martin Quinn and now Bishop Anthony Justs were two visionary pastors for whom I worked. They encouraged me to take initiatives, one of which was a home-based learning program that was modeled on my Bowie experience. As I note later in this book, I facilitated one of the groups, and over the years that we met its members became my dearest friends and teachers. Much of what I write here was birthed in those countless evening sessions.

Another influential member of that parish staff was Rev. Gerard Creedon, now a highly regarded pastor in northern Virginia, who continually advocated for social justice as an essential component of adult faith formation.

I am also grateful to Dr. David Thomas who for years invited me to teach each summer in his graduate program in Adult Faith Formation and Family Ministry at Regis University in Denver. It was there that I honed much of my later thinking on adult education theory and practice.

As the Representative for Adult Education at the United States Conference of Catholic Bishops, I was greatly aided and influenced by my colleagues on the National Advisory Committee on Adult Religious Education (NACARE). In particular, I am indebted to Maureen Shaughnessy, S.C., and Matt Hayes, both of who chaired the committee and enabled it to have a major influence on adult faith formation in the country. They modeled what adult educators should be.

In my role as Executive Director of the NCCL, I was blessed to have an Adult Faith Formation team chaired by Jack McBride that continually challenged me to keep the adult education agenda front and center.

In developing this book's Appendix materials, I consulted a number of colleagues whom I admire and have worked with over many years. They include Ed Gordon; Sr. Janet Schaeffler, O.P.; Dan Mulhall; Rev. David Loftus; Rev. Berard L. Marthaler, O.F.M. Conv.; Sr. Angela Ann Zukowski, M.H.S.H.; Dr. Michael Steier; David Riley; Mark Nuehring, and Jim Schellman. I am grateful to them not only for their kind assistance with this book but also for being such great friends and colleagues over the years.

Finally, I wish to thank my editor Eileen Ponder of Ave Maria Press who guided me through the writing process and who edited the manuscript with wonderful deftness and grace.

Neil A. Parent

CHAPTER 1

The Adult as Christian Disciple and Lifelong Learner

The Critical Importance of Adult Faith Formation

Near the end of *Consuming Religion,* Vincent Miller's impressive analysis of consumerism's destructive effects on religion, he declares, "Catholicism desperately needs adult education on a scale that is daunting."[1] For Miller, today's voracious consumerism is robbing Catholics of their ability to be transformed by the Church's beliefs and symbols. Consequently, he sees the need for a massive educational effort to reconnect believers with the richness, wisdom, and power of their Catholic tradition.

While Miller's is one of the more alarming voices to call for a serious commitment to adult faith formation, it is by no means the first. In recent decades the Church has published an impressive array of documents that call for adult faith formation to be given top priority in its catechetical ministry. The most quoted passage in this regard originated with the 1971 *General Catechetical Directory* and has been repeated in virtually every major catechetical document since. The passage reads:

Catechesis for adults, since it deals with persons who are capable of an adherence that is fully responsible, must be considered the chief form of catechesis. All the other forms, which are indeed always necessary, are in some way oriented to it.[2]

In 1999, the United States Catholic Bishops sought to boost adult faith formation by issuing *Our Hearts Were Burning Within Us: A Pastoral Plan for Adult Faith Formation in the United States (OHWB)*. The document called for a renewed commitment to adult faith formation in parishes and dioceses, especially in terms of leadership development and the allocation of adequate resources. Despite the considerable effort that went into the plan's development and implementation, however, most church officials today would probably admit that we have barely scratched the surface of what needs to be done.

At the same time, those officials would agree that there is a lot of adult learning going on in many, if not most, parishes. Activities such as adult initiation ministries, retreats, Sunday liturgy, intergenerational gatherings, special programs for those with disabilities, leadership development, and sacramental preparation programs for parents demonstrate a commitment to adult faith formation. Still, these activities, however good and important, do not add up to our arriving at a critical sense of urgency that compels us to drop our old habits and seriously address the challenges of adult faith formation as called for in our major catechetical documents.

Why the urgency? The bottom line is this: The world is rapidly changing, and Catholic adults are changing with it. Catholics, like other Christians, are feeling less duty bound to institutional religion. According to the 2009 American Religious Identification Survey report, denominational affiliation in the United States is slipping in importance. The only group that grew in every state since the 2001 survey was people saying that they had "no" religion. This group has now reached 15 percent of the population, with Christians dropping from 86 percent in 1999 to 76 percent today.

The Church today has to prove itself on its own merits. It has to offer Catholics something uniquely desirable, a spiritual enrichment and way of life that is not attainable elsewhere. And unless it does this by reaching out to them, stirring their religious imaginations, and mentoring them into an authentic, fulfilling Catholic way of life, it will find itself with increasingly empty churches.

Empty churches also translate into the Church's depleted ability to carry out its core mission of making disciples of all nations.[3] What is especially serious about this is that the Church exists for mission. In *Evangelii Nuntiandi*, Pope Paul VI wrote:

> Evangelization is in fact the grace and vocation proper to the Church, her deepest identity. She exists in order to evangelize, that is to say, in order to preach and teach. [4]

Adult faith formation's critical role in the Church's evangelizing mission can be seen from its goals and tasks as identified in the major catechetical documents. The *National Directory for Catechesis* pulls together these contributions into the following synthesis:

THE GOALS OF ADULT CATECHESIS

Adult catechesis has three major goals (cf. *OHWB*, nos. 67–73).

1. It invites and enables adults "to acquire an attitude of *conversion to the Lord*" (*Adult Catechesis in the Christian Community [ACCC]*, no. 36). This attitude views the Christian life as a gradual transformation in Christ, in which the Christian takes on the mind of Christ, trusts in the Father's love, accepts the Spirit's guidance in searching out and obeying God's will, and seeks holiness of life within the Church. It fosters a baptismal spirituality in which the

Christian's faith in Jesus is continuously deepened through participation in the sacraments, the works of charity and justice, and the prayer life of the Church.

2. Catechesis for adults helps them make "a conscious and firm decision to live the gift and choice of faith through *membership in the Christian community*" (*ACCC*, no. 37). It fosters active participation in the Church as it is realized in families, small faith-based communities, parishes, dioceses, and the communion of saints. It helps adults develop a deeper sense of their cooperation with the Holy Spirit for the mission of the Church in the world, and for its internal life as well.

3. Catechesis for adults helps them become "more willing and able to be a *Christian disciple in the world*" (*ACCC*, no. 38). It enables adult disciples to accept their rightful place in the Church's mission to evangelize, to hear the cry for justice, to promote unity among Christians, and to bear witness to the salvation won by Jesus Christ for all.

THE TASKS OF ADULT CATECHESIS

The general task of adult catechesis is to "propose the Christian faith in its entirety and in its authenticity, in accordance with the Church's understanding. It must give priority to the proclamation of salvation, drawing attention to the many challenges to living a Christian life posed by American society and culture. It must introduce adults to a faith-filled reading of Sacred Scripture and the practice of prayer" (*General Directory for Catechesis* [GDC], no. 175). In particular, the major tasks of adult catechesis are as follows:

*   To promote the formation and development of life in the Risen Christ through the sacraments, the prayer life of the Church, works of charity and justice, retreats, and spiritual direction.

- To promote evangelization as the means of bringing the Good News to all states of humanity (cf. *Evangelii Nuntiandi*, no. 18).

- To educate toward the development of an informed moral conscience.

- To clarify religious and moral questions.

- To clarify the relationship between the Church and the world, especially in light of the Church's social doctrine.

- To develop the rational foundations of the faith and demonstrate the compatibility of faith and reason.

- *"To encourage adults to assume [their baptismal] responsibility for the Church's mission and to be able to give Christian witness in society"* (GDC, no. 175).

- To develop creative ways through which to interest adults in and encourage them to take advantage of the various programs of enrichment and spiritual development being offered.[5]

In addition to the above tasks, several other reasons for urgency in developing better adult faith formation strategies deserve our attention. **One reason** is the need to equip parents and other adults to successfully hand on the faith to children. Family life is filled with "teachable moments" that parents can and must seize upon to nurture their children's religious imaginations and understanding. But they also need to be able to address honestly and informatively the kinds of thorny questions and statements that children, especially teenagers, often raise about the faith. "Why do we have to go to church when none of my friends have to go?" "I don't understand why the Church won't let Uncle Harry marry his friend, Dan. They love each other." "It's mean and stupid that the Church won't let us girls become priests."

As best they can, parents need to provide answers to such questions that are informed by the Church's teachings. And this does not mean merely dissecting the faith intellectually for their children. Rather, they need to explain the faith in ways that demonstrate their love for it and for the Church that expresses that faith. This would be true even if they themselves were struggling with their own understandings of certain Church teachings. Personal witness of the faith is an essential component of catechesis. As Pope Paul VI noted, "Modern man [sic] listens more willingly to witnesses than to teachers, and if he does listen to teachers, it's because they are witnesses."[6]

The simple fact is that if we cannot adequately explain and personally demonstrate "the reason for [our] . . . hope" to our children, they will be less inspired to follow in our spiritual footsteps.[7] Indeed, the recent *National Study of Youth and Religion* identified the beliefs and faith practices of parents as having the most influence on the beliefs and practices of their children. Bishop Blasé Cupich of Rapid City, South Dakota, expressed it this way at a symposium exploring effective ways to hand on the faith:

> The adult community must be able to demonstrate to young people not only that they have a grasp of the faith but that they are grasped by it.[8]

A second reason for giving more urgency to adult faith formation is that the Christian faith is, for the most part, an adult faith. Much of what it takes to understand the faith—not just with one's head but also with one's heart—can be dealt with adequately only in adulthood.

If the catechetical process stops in early adolescence, many adults are left without an adequate catechetical formation with which to address the kinds of questions and issues that invariably crop up in adulthood, such as the meaning and value of life, the problem of suffering, the moral implications of one's actions, and the longing for transcendence. These and many other issues take on increasing catechetical relevance as one journeys through adulthood.

Related to this is the fact that abstract reasoning, which is so important to mature faith, does not fully develop until the teen years. And that, unfortunately, is just when catechesis ends for so many Catholics. This means that many adult Catholics were never adequately introduced to an understanding of the Church's metaphorical and symbolic language, which is an important theological tool for probing the faith more deeply.

St. Anselm said that theology is faith seeking understanding. While most adults would not see themselves as theologians, they do indeed practice theology as they seek to understand through the eyes of faith the myriad of issues that crop up in their lives. Adult faith formation helps equip them for this important task.

Tod Brown, the Bishop of Orange, California, underscored this very point in a recent pastoral letter to the Catholics of his diocese. "When was the last time you studied your Catholic faith?" he asked his flock. "You can't build your adult faith on a foundation of childish faith."[9] Bishop Brown expressed in a religious way what Robert Maynard Hutchins, the educational philosopher and former president of the University of Chicago, said about learning in general: "Most of the important things that a human being ought to know cannot be comprehended in youth."

A third reason for comprehensive adult faith formation is the rapidly expanding ministerial role of the laity. As Pope Paul VI recognized more than thirty years ago, "the laity feel themselves called to work with their pastors in the service of the ecclesial community for its growth and life, by exercising a great variety of ministries according to the grace and charisms which the Lord is pleased to give them."[10]

Today, adults are being asked increasingly to carry out ministerial tasks as the need arises in their parishes. These ministers need to be credible representatives of the Church, capable of exercising their ministry effectively for the building up of the body of Christ. Adult faith formation is a key means by which the gifts and charisms of adults can be nurtured and empowered for ministry.

Fourth, the growth of an authentic parish community is bound up with the development of an effective adult faith formation ministry. According to the Vatican's International Council for Catechesis, "A fully Christian community can exist only when a systematic catechesis of all its members takes place and when an effective and well-developed catechesis of adults is regarded as the *central task* in the catechetical enterprise."[11]

As we shall see in the next chapter, adult faith formation and the parish community are like linked organs, each nourishing the other. Without a healthy parish community, adult faith formation will have a stunted development. And without good adult faith formation, a parish will never grow to its full potential.

Fifth and finally, the Church needs to engage adults vigorously in the pursuit of learning not only for their sake, but also for its sake. The Church is both an *ecclesia docens* (a teaching church) and an *ecclesia discens* (a learning church). As it has done through the ages, the Church must continually adapt to different times, cultures and circumstances in proclaiming the Good News. It must also unceasingly seek to renew itself, to be ever more faithful to its calling.

The Church's ability to make these changes largely depends upon its ability to learn from information and critique originating outside the echelons of top leadership. A well-informed laity can serve this important role and greatly help the Church in its ongoing process of adjustment and conversion.

In an increasingly complex and globalized society, the Church will need to rely more and more upon an educated laity to help it know how best to carry out and stay faithful to its Gospel mandate. If only for this reason, adult faith formation is absolutely integral to the life and mission of the Church.

The accomplishment of all the above tasks is dependent upon the Church helping its adult members understand that discipleship in Jesus necessitates a lifelong commitment to learning in the faith. Indeed, the very word *disciple* means *learner*. To be a Christian disciple is to be a learner of Jesus, the master teacher.

The goal of this discipleship, as Paul writes in his letter to the Ephesians, is "to grow to the full maturity of Christ."[12] Elsewhere, he says that we Christians "have the mind of Christ"; that is to say, we assume his attitudes, his way of thinking, his way of relating to others, especially to the poor and outcasts.[13] These are aspects of discipleship, of learning in the faith that we will never outgrow.

Who Are Today's Catholic Adults?

The Church's reasons for making adult faith formation its top catechetical priority are both sweeping and compelling, but they fail to tell us anything specific about those we seek to serve here in the United States. Yet, it is the target audience that makes all the difference when it comes to any catechetical endeavor.

Let's look at some of the facts regarding Catholics in the United States. According to the 2008 Pew Religious Landscape Survey, Catholics make up 23.9 percent of the U.S. population.[14] And while nearly one in three Americans (31 percent) were raised Catholic, fewer than one in four (24 percent) describe themselves as Catholic today. What this tells us is that we are not doing a good enough job of holding on to our members.

Dean Hoge, who until his death in September 2008 was professor of the sociology of religion at The Catholic University of America, long maintained that while the Catholic population in the United States shows some modest growth, the reason has more to do with immigration than with the attraction and retention of members. Were it not for the Hispanic immigration into this country, he asserted, the Catholic Church would show a decline in numbers, much like the mainline Protestant churches have done for years. Indeed, according to the National Council of Churches' 2009 *Yearbook of American and Canadian Churches*, membership in the Catholic Church declined by 398,000 members since the publication of the 2008 *Yearbook*.

The truth is that Americans, while maintaining a fairly strong religious self-identity, are becoming less inclined to express that identity through church affiliation. For example, a recent report from the Evangelical Lutheran Church in America, the country's largest Lutheran denomination, states that its membership has fallen for the sixteenth consecutive year. At its 2008 meeting, the Southern Baptist Convention expressed concern over its declining numbers. And even some of the high-flying evangelical mega churches have begun to show cracks in their members' allegiance.[15]

For years we have known that the church attendance and religious attitudes of Catholics were approximating those of mainstream America. In the Pew survey, only 42 percent of Catholics reported attending religious services at least once a week, compared to a 39 percent national average. And that number drops precipitously to 15 percent when it comes to Millennial Catholics (ages eighteen to twenty-five), according to a separate 2005 survey of U.S. Catholics. In that survey, 95 percent of the Millennials said that you can be a good Catholic without going to Mass every week. William V. D'Antonio, one of the researchers, concluded in an accompanying article that, "It will take all the wisdom Church leaders can muster to communicate with tomorrow's laity."[16] This does not exactly sound hopeful for those of us who want to work with adult learners.

When it comes to religious beliefs, clear differences are emerging between how younger Catholic adults and older ones think about their faith, particularly in terms of sexual mores. At the same time, younger Catholics are just a likely as older ones to rate helping the poor, belief in the resurrection, and the sacraments as being very important to their faith. The key issue here is that younger Catholic adults are more likely to make up their own minds about what is important to their faith.

In words coined by cultural anthropologist Clifford Geertz, today's younger Catholic adults are "holding religious views rather than being held by them."[17]

For years, bishops, pastors, and other Church leaders have called for more and better catechesis to stem the trend of "cafeteria-style Catholicism," where members select the doctrines they want and discard the rest. These leaders decry the "lost generations" of Catholics who suffered through what in their view was horrendously poor, content-less catechesis. As they see it, it's no wonder that young people aren't attending Mass and following the Church's teachings: They simply don't know the fundamentals of their faith.

There is certainly some truth in their contentions. But, as is the case in most matters of human behavior, issues are never quite as clear-cut as they seem. For instance, in the study reported in the *National Catholic Reporter* (*NCR*), Jim Davidson, another member of the 2005 research team, observed that the research doesn't demonstrate a connection between religious illiteracy and dissent. "Dissent is not so much a result of a lack of understanding," he wrote, "as it is a disagreement with specific teachings that lay people do not believe are central to their faith."[18] In other words, more Catholics are selecting their own criteria as to what it means to be Catholic.

Where did such a mindset come from? How did we go from a Church prior to Vatican II in which most adult Catholics seemingly complied with Church teaching to where we are today, with most Catholics constructing their own religious identities?

Before attempting to shed some light on this question, I should note that these changing attitudes do not characterize all segments of the U.S. Catholic population. As several writers have pointed out, there is a smaller but significant group of Catholics who remain vitally committed to Catholic identity and to Catholic orthodoxy, as they define it.[19] However, since the focus of this book is on the vast majority of Catholics, whose views are reflected in the national studies, I will mainly have them in mind as I proceed.

What's Impacting Catholic Adult Thinking?

Answers to the above question are not easy to come by, if for no other reason than there are so many influences on today's believers. But available research and social analysis offer us some insight.

Michele Dillon and Paul Wink, two researchers who have traced religious belief, practice, and change across decades, point to a spiritual marketplace greatly expanded since the 1960s, citing it as one of the reasons why it is now easier for Americans to choose among a spectrum of spiritual practices and beliefs.[20] You do not have to be a researcher, however, to see firsthand what they are talking about.

Walk into to any Barnes and Noble or Borders bookstore and you will find hundreds of titles on a vast array of topics representing each of the world's major religions. And this doesn't include the shelves devoted to atheism, new age, paganism, and the occult. And then there is the Internet, with its virtually limitless access to information on all aspects of faith and religion. Wondering if Buddhist meditation is right for you? Just Google it. Want the Pope's latest encyclical? Go to the Vatican's website. Interested in having messages of spiritual wisdom regularly e-mailed you? Subscribe to Beliefnet.com.

Robert Wuthnow, a religion sociologist at Princeton University, sees that this information overload leaves young adults with no recourse but to improvise. As a result, they often form opinions about religion more through mutual influence than through formal teaching. He finds, too, that they are giving primary weight to their own experience in some aspects of belief. For example, he found that two-thirds of young adults in their twenties and thirties opt for personal experience as the best way to understand God. Only one-fourth of those he surveyed opted for Church doctrine.[21]

Vincent Miller, whom I quoted at the beginning of this chapter, worries that our rampant consumer-driven commoditization of virtually everything has influenced believers to regard even religious symbols and beliefs as "things" to be used as one chooses. (A commodity is anything that can be bought, sold or exchanged. It stands alone, apart form any context of broader meaning.) In a religious context, this means that a symbol, such as a cross, can serve either as a dramatic reminder of Jesus' paschal mystery or simply as neck jewelry. It all depends on the user's views.

Or in the case of doctrine, one could, for example, without a broader understanding of the Church's "consistent ethic of life," pick and choose among the various teachings that comprise it. For example, depending upon one's views, one could be against abortion but ignore the Church's teachings on, say, capital punishment, euthanasia, or war. Or vice-versa.

Another problem with viewing religion through consumerist lenses is that we begin to understand or define the laity as consumers of religion, and the clergy as its providers. Religion then becomes the action that takes place between the providers and the consumers. This view of religion sets up a harmful co-dependency between clergy and laity, one that severely hinders effective adult faith formation and the flowering of mature faith for all believers.

Clearly, today's Catholics have different attitudes about beliefs and practices than did their counterparts a generation ago. This is especially so with younger adults who are deciding for themselves what they believe and how they live that belief. But while they may disagree with some Church teachings, they are generally content to identify themselves as Catholics. As sociologist of religion Grace Davies notes, adults today are increasingly standing at some distance from their inherited religion yet still maintaining an affectionate identification with it.

John Hall, a British adult Christian educator, contends that in today's "mixed theological economy," choice in beliefs and practices is a necessity that confronts every believer. The fact of the matter is that churches no longer have a near-exclusive hold on their members' religious attention, as they once did. Today, a wide range of religious information and values compete for believers' attention. And this fact, says Hall, calls for change in the relationship between teaching and learning: "Teaching must now enable learning but not control it. The teacher is the minister to the learner."[22]

Faith Learning Engages the Whole Person

In a way, the Church's entire catechetical effort can be seen as positioned between two New Testament questions. The first is the one posed by Nathanial to Phillip: "Can anything good come from Nazareth?" The second is the question Jesus asks his disciples: "Who do you say that I am?"[23]

Answering the first question is at the center of the Church's mission. From day one, it has proclaimed that something good—indeed, something wonderful—has came out of Nazareth, namely Jesus, Son of God. The heart of the Church's evangelization and catechesis for two thousand years has been to present Jesus in such a way that hearers are ultimately drawn into communion with him.

And that is precisely where the second question comes in. To reach communion with Jesus, we have to discover and acknowledge who Jesus is for ourselves. The Church can't answer the question for us; only we as individuals can answer it.

What is more, having all the information in the world about Jesus won't alone enable us to answer the question in a way that matters. The answer that matters is not simply an intellectual assent, but rather the commitment of our whole person to link our destiny to that of Jesus.

This means that adult religious education is about more than expanding one's understanding of the faith, however important that is. It also means helping the learner attain deeper spiritual wisdom, a wisdom born of one's entire being—the head, heart, and hands, as educators are fond of saying.

Reaching people's hearts, however, is no easy task. Modern culture has so many lures that the heart is often hijacked by far inferior goods than what the Gospel offers.

Culture's Impact on the Heart

There is an ancient proverb that says, "A fish will be the last creature to discover water." What this means is that the fish is so enveloped by and dependent upon water that it doesn't even realize the water is there.

In many ways, culture has that kind of influence on us. We are so much a part of it that we don't realize the extent to which culture shapes our attitudes, ideas, and values—virtually our way of being in this world. This is why Pope John Paul II said, "A faith which does not become culture is a faith which has not been thoroughly received, not fully lived out."[24] He saw full well the interconnection between a supportive culture and a fully lived faith.

When a culture does not support the values of a people's religion, it is much more difficult for them to live their faith. As Jesuit theologian Michael Paul Gallagher puts it, the dominant culture "kidnaps their imagination in trivial ways and therefore leaves them unfree for revelation—or more precisely, for the hearing from which faith comes (cf. Romans 10:17)."[25]

Culture can certainly affect our ability to better understand our faith. But its deepest impact, as Gallagher asserts, is on our imaginative level, below the surface, where we hardly notice how we are being influenced. And where a culture like ours in the United States can be most corrosive to our faith is its subversion of our God-given longings by hijacking them for purposes of consumerism.

In the fifth century, the great St. Augustine wrote, "You have created us for yourself, O God, and our hearts will not rest until they rest in you." It is precisely this restlessness that keeps us longing, moving toward God. It lets us know that God is our true home, our ultimate destiny. When culture hijacks this restlessness through a consumerism that has us endlessly buying "stuff" to temporarily satiate our yearnings—our innate hunger for God—we are diverted from a truer path to God.

I recently came across an alleged parable of Jesus that appears in one of the apocryphal gospels. I believe that the parable, despite it questionable authorship, speaks eloquently to the point under discussion.

> Jesus said: "There went forth two men to sell apples. The one chose to sell the peel of the apple for its weight in gold, caring nothing for the substance of the apples. The other desired to give the apples away, receiving only a little bread for his journey. But men bought the peel of the apples for its weight in gold, caring nothing for him who was joyful to give to them, but also even despising him.[26]

What this apocryphal parable says to me is that instead of accepting the Good News, which is freely given and the answer to the deepest longings of our hearts, we seek instead to satisfy these longings with things that are less fulfilling, mere "peelings" of the real thing. We are often even willing to pay lots of money for these "peelings," which can only briefly quench our longings.

Madison Avenue understands this all too well. It knows that we want to be attractive, loved, happy, and fulfilled. It knows that we want to be free of the fears and anxieties that sometimes cripple us from living freely and nobly. And so it lures us with things that seem to offer answers to our longing for something more out of life. It parades before us countless ads of people happy because of a new car, age-defying beauty treatments, or the advice of a celebrity guru. The ad suggests that fulfillment is easily within reach. You just have to pay for it. And, unfortunately, we too often take the bait.

In an effort to make ourselves happy and fulfilled, we resort to buying lots of things, some of which are quite expensive. But the satisfaction that these things bring doesn't last, and the longing starts all over again. These things are not bad in themselves, but they can create a disconnect with our deeper selves, with the longings of our hearts. These longings are meant by God to lead us to him and not to be diverted into consumerist substitutes.

What does all this mean for adult faith formation? It means, first of all, that we are working with adults, especially young ones, who are becoming increasingly independent in their faith beliefs and practices. It means that these adults live in a culture of choice in which many spiritual paths compete for their attention. It means that the decisions they make regarding a particular path are often based more on the experience they derive from their choice than on theological grounds. And it means that they live in a culture that is constantly bombarding them with superficial things, mere peelings, which can subvert their quest to satisfy their deepest human longings through religion.

In light of this, adult faith formation is not a ministry that can content itself with an exclusive programmatic response. First of all, the numbers of adults that attend adult faith formation classes are minuscule compared to the overall adult population. Second, if today's adults are going to be reached at all, they will have to be reached first and foremost on the level of their religious imagination. This is where the power of faith resides.

Gallagher reminds us that Cardinal Newman insisted that issues of belief arise from the heart rather than the intellect. As Newman wrote in his *Grammar of Assent*, "The heart is commonly reached not through the reason, but through the imagination."[27]

This is not to discount the importance of religious content in the adult faith formation process. But it is to suggest, as every experienced adult educator knows, that adults are free to choose to attend what is being offered or not. And unless we can appeal to something within them that stirs their feelings, their imagination, their sense of need, they are not going to attend.

Furthermore, adult faith formation efforts will necessarily have to enter into the culture of the adult community. We cannot ignite people's religious imaginations by standing apart from the very context in which they live. As Gallagher puts it, "Religious anemia is produced when the receiver encounters only the conventional or complacent externals of an institution, and when the communicators of faith fail to enter respectfully into the culture of the receiver."[28]

The simple fact we should keep in mind is that Jesus taught in and through the culture of his day. We need to adapt lessons from his teaching methods in order to reach our contemporaries today.

Much of what we will talk about in the remainder of this book will deal with how we might connect with today's adults, who they are, and where they are. This is not and cannot be a task of the adult faith formation minister alone; it is a task of the entire parish community. And it is the faith community to which we now turn our attention.

Questions for Reflection

1. Of the tasks that have been identified for adult faith formation, which ones stand out for you as the most critical today?

2. In 1958, weekly Catholic church attendance was about 75 percent. What do you think are the primary causes for the significant drop in attendance?

3. How do you feel about Catholics making up their own minds about what is essential to the faith?

4. What would you do to reestablish a stronger sense of Church affiliation among younger Catholic adults?

5. What do you see in our culture that is supportive of our deeper spiritual longings?

6. What in this chapter strikes you as having the most profound implications for adult faith formation?

CHAPTER 2

The Parish as Context for Adult Faith Formation

Soil

When I first entered the field of catechesis, I did so as a newly appointed director of adult education in a northern Virginia parish. While I had a master's degree in theology, my experience in catechesis was limited. I decided, therefore, to seek the guidance of a friend of mine who was a priest and director of adult education for a neighboring archdiocese.

We spent the better part of a morning discussing how I might go about developing an adult education program in my parish. But of all the things I remember about that conversation, the one that stands out the most for me, and the one that proved most useful over the years, was this: "Neil, you've got to focus on building a parish culture that encourages and supports adult faith formation. Everything else depends upon that."

In later years, when I served as the representative for adult education at the United States Conference of Catholic Bishops, I frequently used the parable of the Sower and the Seed in workshops on adult faith formation to illustrate the vital connection between parish culture and adult programming.[29] In order to dramatize the point, I would often portray in front of the participants a sower with a bag of seeds hanging from his side, broadcasting them left and right.

I would tell them that the seed represents the programs that they want to offer, and the soil represents the parish. Just as seed cannot grow on rocky soil, neither can an adult faith formation program do well without the fertile soil of a good parish environment. "If people's experience of the parish is poor," I would ask the participants, "what reason would they have to turn out for a program you are offering? Like it or not, their poor experience of the parish will be projected onto your programs." They got my point. And they knew from experience that it was true.

As I traveled the country doing workshops on adult faith formation, participants often approached me saying that they had tried to implement the principles we were discussing, but they could not make any real progress. In those instances, I learned to say, "Tell me about your parish." Sure enough, the person would outline a tale of woe about his or her parish: dreadful liturgies (especially homilies), continual focus on money issues, little or no social outreach, lack of any real sense of community, and so on.

What is important to realize is that parish structures and practices are continually shaping its members' faith in all that it does—one way or another. Sunday liturgy is the most notable example. When liturgies are well prepared, the homily stimulating and informative, and the music uplifting, most attendees would probably give the parish high marks. But if the liturgy is poor, you can bet that the parishioners generally hold an unfavorable view of the parish.

The liturgy, however, is only one way, albeit a very important way, that parish members get formed in the faith. All of the parish's activities and communications coalesce over time to imprint on its members a strong impression of what comprises the Catholic way of life. Think of the humble parish bulletin, with its information about what the parish is doing (or not doing) to serve the needs of its members and those in the wider community. For many people, the bulletin and Sunday Mass comprise the public face of the parish, and by these, people judge it.

In my own parish, Our Lady Queen of Peace in Arlington, Virginia, the bulletin reminds us weekly of what's going on with our sister parish in Haiti, with efforts to address needs of affordable housing, with food collection for the poor, with speakers and courses for faith development of all ages, with ministry to the gay and lesbian community, and so on. In this parish, an adult would not have to take a single course to understand that to be Catholic is to put one's faith into action, especially on behalf of the most needy. In essence, one absorbs one's Catholic faith, breathes it in, as it were, by participating in a thriving parish community.

The fact of the matter is that the lived experience of participating in the life of the parish community has a far greater impact on adult faith formation than any program possibly could. For example, one may proclaim from the pulpit or teach in a classroom that social justice is a constitutive part of the Gospel, which is a key Catholic teaching that emerged in the aftermath of Vatican II. But if the parish budget allocates little money to help others, if there is virtually no organized social outreach ministry, or if social justice issues are rarely addressed from the pulpit or seen in the bulletin, the stronger message to parishioners is that social justice is not that important to one's faith. How could it be? It barely surfaces in the life of the community.

Pastors and others concerned about adult faith formation must continually ask themselves what messages are being transmitted to parishioners through the various activities and communication channels of the parish. This even includes the buildings. What kind of space is given over to adult faith formation, to hospitality, to other important aspects of gathering, celebrating, and empowering Catholic Christian life? All aspects of the parish play an important role in the formation of Catholics, whatever their age.

A good way to think about this is to imagine a few strangers coming to your parish for a few weeks while conducting business in town. Just from their attending the Sunday liturgies, looking over the parish bulletin, perhaps dropping in on one or two activities, how would they describe what it means to be Catholic, based on what they had experienced? What sense would they have about how the Catholic faith is being lived out? Catholics can and do have different understandings of and feelings for what it means to be Catholic simply by virtue of how they have been socialized into the faith through parish life.

There is nothing more important to the well-being of adult faith formation than a vibrant, mission-focused parish community. The *General Directory for Catechesis* puts it this way:

> Catechetical pedagogy will be effective to the extent that the Christian community becomes a point of concrete reference for the faith journey of individuals. This happens when the community is proposed as a source, *locus* and means of catechesis. Concretely, the community becomes a visible place of faith witness. It provides for the formation of its members. It receives them as the family of God. It constitutes itself as the living and permanent environment for growth in the faith.[30]

That last sentence is the all-important one. Virtually everything needed for an effective adult faith formation ministry hinges on the parish's being an "environment for growth in the faith." Episcopalian educator and researcher Jean Haldane would agree. She refers to the local congregation as the "laboratory for the Kingdom."[31] Along with the family, she sees the parish as the place where we learn to live the Gospel values Jesus identified with God's kingdom. But if parishes are to be effective as a laboratory for the Kingdom, it is vitally important that they regularly evaluate how well they are carrying out that mission.

Several years ago I was invited to contribute to the development of a parish self-assessment program.[32] The idea behind the project was to create materials and a mechanism that would enable parishes to evaluate how well they were doing in seven major ministry areas, such as catechesis, prayer and worship, community building, and justice and charity. Following the self-evaluation, parishes could then make plans for improving in areas where they had judged themselves deficient. My task was to develop the list of criteria statements for effective catechetical ministry.

I mention this because unless parishes regularly assess their performance, they will not know in what areas they may be underserving their members. And given the interlocking nature of ministries, deficiency in one area will invariably cause problems in others. If community building, social outreach, or family ministry is underperforming, adult faith formation will suffer. Adult faith formation cannot thrive on its own. It needs the rich, fertile soil of a good parish in which to grow and blossom.

As I noted in the preceding chapter, increasing numbers of Catholics are following their own spiritual path, apart from any connection with a faith community. One problem with this is that without the benefit of the broader perspective that community brings, one could easily lose one's way. Many Gospel values are counter-intuitive and, as a result, countercultural. Jesus tells us that we must lose our life in order to save it, that the poor will inherit the earth, and that the last shall be first. The parish community serves as a teacher and helps us stay focused on what is right and true within our cultural vortex of conflicting values.

Culture can and frequently does deafen our ability to hear the Word of God. One speaker at a workshop on adult faith development expressed it this way: "Religion . . . continues to span culture and helps us see from the perspective of community in ways that our individualistic cultural spectacles often lose sight of."[33]

An important benefit of our being part of a community of faith is that we can help each other respond more faithfully to Jesus' call to discipleship. I often sit in church amazed and humbled by the many good works being done by my fellow parishioners. Their example and their open invitation to join them in their ministries motivate me to want to live a more committed Catholic life. And motivation, as we shall see, is an essential ingredient of effective adult faith formation.

Community

In *Habits of the Heart*, Robert Bellah's landmark study on American values, he noted that American Catholics identify the faith primarily with what goes on in the family and the local parish, and are less influenced by the pronouncements of bishops and the pope.[34] This is not hard to understand. For most Catholics in the United States, the local parish has always been the face of the Church. And, in many respects, this is as it should be. The New Testament identifies the church (*ecclesia*) with the local community of believers.[35]

Regrettably, however, many U.S. Catholics do not view or experience the parish as a true community. As I noted in the last chapter, growing numbers of Catholics tend to see the parish as the place where they go to "consume" religion. And too often the parish obliges by acting as kind of sacramental service station, devoid of any energizing vision or community spirit.

Research shows, however, that what makes a congregation, large or small, attractive is a sense of community. People of all ages, says researcher Robert Wuthnow, want to feel that they are part of a community.[36] Even megachurches, with their vast numbers at Sunday services, get high marks for creating a sense of community among members. According to the Institute for Studies of Religion, they do this by effectively breaking down the congregation into smaller groupings that meet regularly.[37] Many Catholic parishes have been working on similar strategies for years with some success.

The research shows that people benefit from being active in their faith communities. They are more likely, for example, to say that they pray, look to God for strength, feel God's presence, and find comfort in their faith if they are active in their faith communities.[38] The Vatican document *Adult Catechesis in the Christian Community* reminds us that "adults do not grow in faith primarily by learning concepts, but by sharing the life of the Christian community."[39]

I once worked for a pastor who wanted to do something dramatic to drive home the point that the parish was to be a community and not just a weekly gathering of worshippers. Eventually he decided to erect a large sign in front of the church, which faced a well-traveled street. The sign read, "Blessed Sacrament Catholic Community, Welcome, Rejoice, and Come In."

As staff members, we were both surprised and pleased that the sign attracted so many non-parishioners. A common remark we heard from these visitors was, "We've never seen a Catholic church with a welcome sign before. It made us think that this is a parish that we would like to join. It has the right spirit." Young adults are especially drawn to parishes that display spirit, enthusiasm, and, as we shall see, a strong mission focus.

I once heard the following story about "spirit" that I think applies here:

> One Sunday morning in a proper New England downtown church, a woman who clearly had come from a different part of town slipped into one of the pews, where she remained very quiet until the sermon. As the preacher launched into his sermon she called out, "Yes, Lord, preach it!" A few minutes later she boomed out a

loud "Amen!" And then a few minutes later she yelled, "Praise Jesus! Praise Jesus!"

By this point an usher had made his way over to her pew, leaned down, and said to her, "Madam, is there something wrong?" "No," she said. "I've just got the spirit!" To which the usher sternly replied, "Well, madam, you certainly didn't get it here."

This is the problem with too many of our parishes. People are not finding "the spirit" there. And for many people today, "spirit" or a spiritually enriching experience, is what they are looking for. Far too many Catholics, especially our Hispanic brothers and sisters, have joined evangelical churches because of their spirit of welcome, inclusiveness, and uplifting preaching and singing.

Getting the right spirit in a Catholic parish is, of course, about more than erecting a welcome sign. The pastor who did that was constantly coming up with ingenious ways to foster a communal spirit, from extending hospitality, to celebrating volunteers, to hosting town hall meetings, to sponsoring large numbers of ministerial and faith development groups. Building a community spirit takes effort, but without it, no effective adult faith formation ministry can grow.

A final point about community. Bear in mind that the kind of community we are talking about is not, in the words of Robert Bellah, a "lifestyle enclave of warm, mutual acceptance."[40] People who are cookie-cutter-alike are hardly in the best position to aid each other's learning. Rather, a Christian community brings together all of Jesus' disciples, regardless of their backgrounds. They might come from all sorts of ethnic and racial backgrounds, spanning a wide range of ages. They might hold widely varying ideas and attitudes about politics and religion. Even so, together they make up the people of God.

This point was driven home to me one Easter Sunday morning. As I pulled into the parish parking lot with my wife and children, I quickly observed that all the parking places were already taken. Since we had rushed to arrive early to get seats, I became upset with the thought that the "twice-a-year Catholics" had somehow beat us out. "Of course they would," I thought. "Mass is not until 10:30 a.m., and those clueless folks probably thought Mass began at 10:00 a.m."

Sure enough, the church was packed with unfamiliar faces, and we ended up squeezed together in a crowd packed at the back of the church. After processing in, the pastor welcomed the congregation and began with these words: "Isn't it wonderful that all of us have come here today to celebrate Jesus' Resurrection. Some of us are here weekly, others of us are not able to come that frequently, and still others of us try at least to be here for Christmas and Easter. But no matter. What is important is that we are all God's children, and today we have come to give glory and praise to God for raising Jesus from the dead."

His words tore through me because I knew that just a few minutes earlier I was harboring "better than thou" thoughts about some of my fellow believers. We are all different, yes, but at the same time we are all God's children. And God loves us all, just as we are.

What we need to keep in mind as adult religious educators is that our differences as God's children will require a smorgasbord of approaches to adult faith development. Not everyone in the community will have the same attraction to liturgy or other church activities. Not everyone will come from the same age group or racial, ethnic, or economic background. Not everyone will think the same way about moral or doctrinal issues. Not everyone will be excited about what religiously excites us. Yet each person deserves the opportunity for growth in faith that best meets with his or her faith needs and style.

Whole Parish

Renowned catechetical leader Maria Harris was fond of saying that it is the whole Church that teaches and the whole Church that learns. The same is true at the parish level. It is the whole parish that teaches, and it is the whole parish that learns.

This understanding about the entire parish community's role as teacher has emerged strongly of late in the development of what is known as Whole Community Catechesis and in derivative programs such as Generations of Faith.[41] As catechetical leaders have grown increasingly frustrated by the shortcomings of classroom-catechesis, they have turned their attention to a more holistic approach to faith formation, one that involves a wide cross-section of parish life—in particular the involvement of parents—to improve catechesis for children.

Intergenerational learning is a major motivator for adults to attend learning sessions. While many adults would not make time to attend a program aimed at them, they will often make time if it means improvement for the formation of their children. Lots of creative ways can be introduced in intergenerational learning that can benefit the parents as well as the children.

When I was serving as director of adult faith formation in my parish, we used to hold annual weekend family retreats at a retreat center in the country. The centerpiece of the retreat was intergenerational learning that took place in a number of formats. Sometimes, children were separated by age groups to discuss a theme while the adults met in groups. On other occasions, adults and children were mixed together in groups. And on still other occasions, families met as units. Single adults, who formed a household of one, were always welcome on the weekend and invited to join with other family groupings. We never ceased to be amazed at how enthusiastically the adults engaged in the learning sessions and what positive evaluations they gave to the experience. For many of them, a special treat was seeing one or more of their children raise questions or give a group report. These adults would often say that they had no idea their children thought about such spiritual matters.

If there is one overriding aspect to a parish community, besides good liturgy, that is crucial to good adult faith formation, it is mission. By this I mean that a parish community has an understanding, a cultural perspective that it does not exist for itself but for the sake of the reign of God. The parish sees itself in mission to bring the Good News to others through word and action. Indeed, as St. Francis of Assisi is alleged to have said, "Preach the Word at all times, and when necessary, use words."

As has been previously noted, too many parishes buy into the religion-as-commodity model and act as if they were spiritual service stations. Each week they gather their members for a little religion and then send them home, fueled for another week away. This is hardly the image Jesus presents of his church. He uses metaphors such as leaven, salt, and light to suggest the transforming power that needs to be present in his disciples. Jesus himself was a mover and shaker. He went out, stirred things up, got things done. And he recruited disciples to do likewise. He was about ushering in the reign of God, and he wanted others to join him in that effort. It is this going out, this doing something for the reign of God, that plays such a important role in adult faith formation. Here's why.

First, the Christian faith is not a set of doctrines or concepts; it is a way of life, a way of being in the world. The only way you can come to a richer and more complete understanding of the faith is to live it, to put it into action, to allow it to stretch you beyond yourself in love to others. A parish community that does not have a rich mission-oriented culture deprives its members of opportunities to grow more deeply in their faith, either by direct involvement or by learning through the example and experience of others. Researcher Robert Wuthnow cites the case of a twenty-nine-year-old male who is now

Presbyterian because his new church gave him an opportunity to serve, whereas his Catholic parish did not.[42]

Second, a mission-oriented parish invariably has more energy coursing through its institutional veins. And this energy is attractive, especially to young adults. Indeed, one of the well-researched reasons for the growth of evangelical megachurches is their emphasis on mission. True, some of it is about proselytizing, but a lot of it is about members helping people in their local neighborhood, in the inner city, or across the ocean.

Some years ago when I served as executive director of the National Conference for Catechetical Leadership, we hosted, along with the William H. Sadlier Publishing Company, a symposium on the priest as empowerer of catechetical ministry. Each of NCCL's member provinces was asked to identify a priest who exemplified a good catechetical leader and empowered others in that ministry.

I noticed many common things about the men who were selected, such as their vision, energy, enthusiasm, dedication, and humility. But one thing that stood out for me was that virtually all of them headed parishes with strong social outreach ministries. As they described their parishes, you heard again and again such references as hosting soup kitchens, sending groups on missions to Mexico, and supporting sister parishes. These were men that understood the close connection between mission and adult faith formation.

Third, involvement in mission is often a stimulus for people's wanting to learn more about the faith. Some years ago, a pastor from the Midwest (whom I cite at greater length later in the book) described to me his many failed attempts to get adult faith formation off the ground in his parish. He finally threw up his hands and turned his attention instead to forming mission groups that would address pressing needs both within and beyond the parish. To his surprise, members of these groups soon began to ask for adult faith formation. It seems that having put their faith into action, they now wanted formal opportunities to reflect upon and learn more from their experiences.

Linking Faith and Life

A parish can impair the faith development of its members if it somehow conveys that it is the primary locus of their encounter with the sacred. What happens at the parish, especially in the celebration of the sacraments, is indeed sacred. But the parish's role is primarily to help its members discover, reverence, and respond to the sacred in their daily lives.

In 1973, James Tunstead Burtchaell, then a theology professor at Notre Dame, wrote the following in his book, *Philemon's Problem: The Daily Dilemma of the Christian*:

> The specific purpose of worship is not to save, but to reveal that there is a God who is at all times saving. Sacraments are not meant to draw one's attention away from secular pursuits, as from a distraction. On the contrary, what they celebrate is the salvific power of common activities performed with uncommon generosity. One draws away from one's work to contemplate it, rather than to forget it. Liturgy does not afford an occasion of retreat, so that one may step aside momentarily and attend to his intimacy with God, which is neglected during those workaday times when he is preoccupied with matters mundane. It was never intended as a refuge from the mundane. It does not offer access to the Father any more immediate than one has elsewhere. Nor does it offer a forum wherein one may remedy her faults and shed her sins. Worship reveals one's Lord to a person, and also reveals his or her own heart to him. It offers no escape from the world, but casts over it the high-intensity brilliance of faith.[43]

What Burtchaell reminds us is that it is daily life that is important in the pursuit of holiness. It is there that God interacts most with us. It is there that we most work out our salvation. The catechetical process has no power to transform unless it can connect with people where they are and how they are.

I am convinced that the great challenge facing us today as adult catechetical leaders is to bridge the gap that too frequently develops between religion and life, where religion is something one does rather than something one lives. Our task as ministers is to help adults realize that they are truly bearers of God's presence and to live in accordance with that understanding.

The great St. Augustine was a masterful teacher who always sought to make an enlightening application of the Christian message to people's lives. In speaking about the eucharist, he expressed it this way: "If therefore you yourselves are the Body of Christ and its members then your own mystery lies on the altar. Be what you see and receive what you are."[44]

A few years ago, I had the opportunity to participate in an international Catholic adult faith formation forum in Thailand. At one point we traveled to Chiangmai in the north of Thailand to visit with Fr. Cyril Niphot Thienvihan, the vicar general of the diocese. He spoke to us about the diocese's ministry to the "village people," a Hmong-like population that migrated across the border from their mountain villages in Burma. He said that the task of evangelizing and catechizing the villagers entails building connections between their everyday lives and the Catholic faith. Religion, he said, is not about giving something extra but about experiencing God in life.

He spoke of how the people in the village see all nature as saturated with the spirit of God. For example, rice is sacred for them and is seen as feminine because it gives life. He explained that the Church draws upon the village people's strong sense of God's spirit in nature in order to help them understand Catholic beliefs. For example, their seeing God's spirit in rice is, he said, in a very real sense, eucharistic. "We help them understand the eucharist through how they already see God's spirit hidden within the very food they eat." He went on to say that rice was also being used to catechize about the paschal mystery of Jesus because its seed dies and is reborn into something that gives life.

The main point that Fr. Cyril kept returning to is that the sacred already exists in people's lives, and the task of religion is to make connections with those sacred dimensions of their lives, not to call their attention elsewhere. "Religion is like a kite," he said, "that must be continually brought down to where people live their lives. It is not something that floats above us or is apart from us."

Michael J. Himes, a professor of theology at Boston College, similarly stresses the need to connect religion with people's lives. He says that "communicating faith is not primarily a matter of supplying propositions and information (although that is part of faith) but rather evoking and naming experiences. The teacher of faith should help his hearers examine their experience and offer categories to them for understanding that experience. Teaching faith is, in a sense, offering people a hermeneutic for interpreting what they experience with and around themselves so that disparate parts of their experience begin to connect and emerge as a meaningful whole."[45]

Discipleship

In the previous chapter I pointed out that to be a disciple of Jesus was to be a lifelong learner. Unfortunately, this is not an understanding that most Catholic adults have about themselves. Yes, they would agree that they are disciples of Jesus; but they would undoubtedly express surprise to learn that the word *disciple* means that they are learners in the faith.

One of the best things a parish can do to support adult faith formation is to create an understanding, a mindset, if you will, among its parishioners that it takes learning in the faith seriously for all ages. The change won't happen overnight, but through ongoing efforts, it will gradually sink into adult members that learning in the faith is both an opportunity and a responsibility of being a disciple of Jesus.

A woman who is a member of the faith-based discussion group that my wife and I belong to, periodically attends adult education offerings at a nearby Baptist church. She has been impressed by the quality of the programs, and has from time to time sent information about them, along with some published sermons of the pastor, to the rest of us in the group.

In one of her e-mail attachments from the church, I read the following: "Ravensworth Baptist Church is an inclusive and welcoming Christian Community where expressing the love of God to all people is central to our worship, study, and service." I like the statement a lot, but the word *study* jumped out at me. There it was, right between *worship* and *service*. How many Catholic parishes would give *study* or *learning* such prominence in its mission? Yet unless we start to think of ourselves and speak of ourselves as learning communities—and, of course, act on that belief—we will never begin to make progress toward having vigorous adult faith formation in our communities.

Adult faith formation either thrives or dies depending upon the quality of a parish's community life. Where a parish's community life is spiritually uplifting, focused on mission, dedicated to connecting faith with the daily lives of its members, and demonstrably committed to discipleship as lifelong learning, adult faith formation should do well. But even a great parish will not be enough to bring about good adult faith formation unless significant planning and human and financial resources are committed to the task. It all comes down to how dedicated a parish is to realizing the vision of discipleship as learning for life.

Questions for Reflection

1. What would you consider to be the top three things a parish can do to support an effective adult catechetical ministry?

2. What, in your view, is the most significant thing a parish can do to hinder effective adult faith formation?

3. What does your parish do well in promoting a spirit of community?

4. If a stranger visited your parish, what adjectives would he or she use to describe it?

5. How would you rate your parish's dedication to mission outside of serving its members?

6. How effectively does your parish link what it does at the parish with the lives of its members?

7. To what degree does your parish promote a sense of itself as a "learning community"?

CHAPTER 3

The Adult as Faith Learner

The literature on the adult as a learner has shown remarkable consistency over the years. Resource after resource describes the same basic dimensions of the adult learner. I draw upon them again here, although I understandably bring a religious perspective to them. I have also added a dimension on learning how to learn because of my strong conviction of its importance.

Key Dimensions of the Adult Learner

ADULTS MAINTAIN THE ABILITY TO LEARN

Research over the past several decades has shown that, contrary to popular opinion, adults maintain a strong ability to learn right up to life's end. The old adage "You can't teach an old dog new tricks" may apply to dogs but definitely not to humans.

Recent research on the human brain, furthermore, shows a surprising amount of neuroplasticity in adults that results from their undertaking new activities.[46] In other words, as adults learn new things or engage in new activities, the brain actually changes, forms new neural passages to help facilitate the process. For example, an adult who undertakes learning a new language, playing a musical instrument, or engaging in meditation will gradually undergo changes in his or her brain structure and functions. The brain does not stop changing at the end of adolescence but continues to transform itself to meet new challenges. God made the human brain for a lifetime of learning and doing; and just as the body benefits from exercise, so, too, does the brain function at its best when engaged regularly in activities that stretch its capabilities.

Still, some adults may not feel that they are any longer able to learn effectively, and they don't want to display their shortcomings in a room of other adults, especially people they know. This attitude poses a challenge to parish catechetical leaders who are trying to attract parishioners to their programs. Warm, personal invitation and attractive promotional material that conveys a non-threatening learning process are steps that can be taken to entice reluctant learners to participate.

Although adults retain a remarkable ability to learn new information and skills throughout their lives, any lack of readiness to learn on their part can short-circuit the process. That comment about old dogs and new tricks is more a matter of attitude than it is of capability. As was noted in the last chapter, much of what a parish should do regarding faith formation is to create a culture that in a variety of ways consistently conveys that learning in the faith is a lifelong endeavor.

If an adult harbors a defeatist, disinterested, or disinclined attitude toward education, not much learning is going to take place. Hence, it is vitally important for adult catechetical leaders to pay close attention to the developmental tasks of adults and to other potential "teachable moments" that can spark adults' interests in learning. We will be looking at some of these issues later in this chapter and in the final chapter, which is devoted to program planning.

ADULTS EXPERIENCE A GRADUAL DECLINE IN PHYSICAL/SENSORY CAPABILITIES

Aging does have some effects upon the speed of learning, but its impact is not dramatic. These effects, however, can be minimized by adults increasing the amount of learning in which they engage. Indeed, older adults who return to college for credit or audit often outperform their younger classmates. They bring a richer background of experience to the discussion and often display more dedication to the task of learning. Besides, the greater depths of wisdom and judgment accrued from navigating life's challenges over decades more than make up for any slowing down of mental processes.

It is also important to note that what may appear as "slowness" in the learning process may have as much to do with time needed for learning integration as it does with physical decline. Adult learners do not bring an empty mind to the classroom. They are filled with experiences and value commitments that have shaped their attitudes over the years. When confronted with new information or ways of seeing or doing things, it takes adults longer to integrate the new information with past understandings, especially if the new information is in conflict with long-held views.

When I was studying adult education in graduate school, one of my professors used to stress the need for designing extra time into the learning process in order for adults to integrate the new information with their current understandings and values. I appreciated his advice and have tried to apply it whenever I could. And I must confess my own aggravation when I am being pushed from activity to activity in a learning situation without the benefit of being able to adequately integrate the new information in ways that benefit me.

When we do not allow adequate time for adults to grapple with their experience, values, and assumptions in light of new information being presented, we are essentially working out of an educational model that says learning is more about absorbing new information than it is about actively confronting it, working with it, and ultimately being changed by it. The latter is obviously a more time-consuming process than the former. But it is also a much more beneficial process—and a necessary one if adult catechesis is to contribute to authentic growth in the faith. In his book, *The Modern Practice of Adult Education*, Malcolm Knowles writes: "The important implication for adult-education practice is the fact that learning is an internal process and that those methods and techniques which involve the individual most deeply in self-directed inquiry will produce the greatest learning."[47]

I have often thought that a failure to respect the long-held values of believers was one of the reasons the implementation of Vatican II decrees met with vehement resistance by some Catholics. This was especially true in the realm of the Church's liturgy with its rich symbolic language that speaks more to the heart than to the head. So many changes were made in such a short amount of time, often without the benefit of adequate educational processes to help believers air their concerns, raise their questions, and express their sense of loss over a form of ritual that they deeply treasured.

In those situations, what learners perhaps wanted and needed to hear most from those describing the coming changes was something like, "I hear your concerns about the proposed changes and what it is that you do not want to lose in the liturgy. Let's see if I can show how what you value most in the current liturgy is being preserved in the new rite." What learners most often want from instructors is a sense that they truly understand and care about their feelings and views on the subject, and that they provide appropriate time in the learning process for them to sort through the issues in their hearts as well as their heads.

Thus far we have focused on the decline in learning speed that affects adults as they age. But there are also other physical factors influencing the learning process that need to be attended to. As adults age, their aural and visual acuity gradually diminish. So does their tolerance for cold rooms, uncomfortable chairs, and long stretches without bathroom breaks. Well-lit rooms with good sound amplification, comfortable seating, and good climate control and frequent breaks are important ingredients for helping adults learn well and keep coming back for more.

ADULTS ARE A HIGHLY DIVERSIFIED GROUP OF INDIVIDUALS, WITH WIDELY DIFFERING PREFERENCES, NEEDS, BACKGROUNDS, LEARNING STYLES, AND SKILLS

Since the emergence of significant adult education theory (sometimes referred to as andragogy) in the middle of the last century and the work done on adult life stages, much attention has been focused on various aspects of adult psychosocial development in relation to the learning process. And perhaps no greater insight about adulthood has emerged from this work than that of the expansive diversity that exists within the adult population.

Over the years, so much attention was paid to the dramatic developmental processes of children and adolescents that, by comparison, adults seemed pretty much the same. Adulthood was seen as a final plateau, an end to the developmental process, a maturity goal having been achieved.

Perhaps this is why. when it comes to adult faith formation, we tend to treat all adults alike. An adult education program is, after all, for adults. But that is one reason why adult faith formation programs often do so poorly with attendance. Programs intended for everyone often appeal to virtually no one. They have no particularity, no identification with identifiable needs and interests. Yet, particularity in adult education is where the seeds of success are planted.

You do not have to do any in-depth research to discover just how diverse we are as adults. The evidence is right before us, if we just take the time to think about it. We are male and female, young and old, experienced and inexperienced, gay and straight, married and single, white collar and blue collar, educated and uneducated, conservative and liberal, religious and not religious, healthy and ill, rich and poor, with disabilities and without disabilities. We are black and white, yellow and brown. We come in all sizes and shapes and speak hundreds of different languages. And that is just for starters.

Working in a large, modern bookstore, as I have from time to time, has left me with an unmistakable impression of just how diverse adult interests and needs are. The spectrum of what readers find interesting, useful, and entertaining is utterly breathtaking. And we are all the better for it, especially when it comes to learning. The spectrum of experiences and insights available in any group of adults is an incredibly rich learning resource that the adult catechetical leader should seize upon for the benefit of the whole group.

On the Sunday following September 11, 2001, I drove to church with one of my brothers, whom I was visiting in another state at the time. He had the car radio tuned to NPR, where someone was interviewing the Muslim chaplain at Georgetown University about the terrible events of the past week. We tuned in too late to hear most of what the chaplain had been saying, but at one point he said to the interviewer, "The one thing we know about God is that God wants diversity."

That thought has stayed with me, and I dwell on it often. Our planet is rich in its biodiversity. There are so many species of insects, plants, and animals that their numbers are uncountable. But it is precisely that diversity that makes our planet healthy and creative. The same is true of people. Pick up any *National Geographic* magazine, and you will see just how different we are as a human race. As was noted earlier, the human family bulges with variety. We think differently, have different tastes and interests, different customs, different ways of viewing reality. But these differences add fuel to the learning fire if we are not threatened by it and can take advantage of it.

There are two lessons that we can draw from our diversity as an adult population. **The first, as has already been mentioned, is that particularity often serves adults best.** That is to say, we need to design programs and do outreach to people who share common interests or needs. It is important when thinking of adult faith formation to think of target groups rather than whole populations.

This, of course, is not a hard and fast rule; it is merely a guiding principle. There are plenty of topics and lots of notable speakers that would have broad appeal across the adult population. But generally, adults are more driven to attend educational programs on a topic that resonates with an interest or need that they have.

One of my first responsibilities when I became the director of adult education in a parish was to work with the single adults that were already meeting on a regular basis. Their interests varied from that of the general adult population in the parish. For example, they wanted to address topics such as commitment, premarital sex, loneliness, life vocation, use of leisure time, and medical ethics. Speakers were brought in each week to help them address these topics. The fact that these young adults not only shared common interests but also had a hand in determining how they best wanted to address them made the program successful.

A second lesson to be learned from the vast diversity within adulthood is to avoid the temptation as pastoral ministers to clone ourselves through the educational process. What I mean by this is that our way of being Catholic, with our high involvement in the activities of the Church, is not everyone's calling. We are not the yardstick by which the faithful practice of Catholicism is measured. The widespread diversity within the adult population means that there is a similar diversity in how to be Catholic.

In *Finnegan's Wake,* James Joyce refers to Catholicism as "Here Comes Everybody." The adult catechetical process is not intended to create a generic Catholic but to help each Catholic develop his or her own unique response to God's call. The learning process is more about helping adults discover their own spiritual path within the Catholic tradition than it is about their being shown the path to take.

It is certainly true that the parish community needs people who are involved with and excited about liturgy and the parish's social outreach efforts. But the vast majority of Catholic adults have major demands on their time outside the parish. There are kids to raise, jobs to master, aging parents to look after, loans to pay off. And when it comes to social outreach, many adult Catholics are already involved in civic and charitable activities.

People's vast differences in tastes and interests pull them in a rich variety of directions that contribute to the building up of God's reign. But they are not activities that necessarily flow from the parish. Still, there will be plenty of parishioners whose interests will be directed more to the parish, and their interests should be cultivated and supported but not seen as somehow better than those who give their time and treasure through other avenues. The purpose of adult faith formation is not to create church-oriented activists but to empower the faithful to build up the Kingdom of God, each in his or her own sphere of activity.

Learning Styles

One of the important ways that adults differ when it comes to education is in terms of their preferred learning styles. Not everyone likes to learn the same way. Some like group process; others don't. Some like to engage the speaker with discussion and questions; others are content to hear what the speaker has to say and draw their own conclusions. Still others are more inclined to want to experience something new and different, while others would feel threatened by learning activities that are unfamiliar to them.

The challenge in adult catechesis is to keep in mind that in any given gathering of learners, there are present multiple preferred learning styles. What this generally means is that if learners do not experience, at least in part, their preferred learning style, they don't feel that good learning took place. A person who comes to a program to hear an expert address a topic, only to find that instead she spends most of her time in small group discussion, is likely to feel cheated as a learner. She did not experience what for her constitutes authentic learning.

In Nikos Kasantzakis's book, *Zorba the Greek*, Zorba listens as his boss expounds:

> "Everything, men, animals, trees, stars, we are all one substance involved in the same terrible struggle. What struggle? . . . Turning matter into spirit."
>
> Zorba scratched his head [and said], "I've got a thick skull, boss, I don't grasp these things easily. Ah, if only you could dance all that you've just said, then I'd understand. . . . Or if you could tell me all that in story, boss."[48]

For Zorba, learning is connected to movement or story. Those are his preferred learning styles, and when they are used, he learns at his best. The same is true for us. We all have our preferred learning styles, and we learn best when we experience our style being used.

Unless the adult catechetical leader is working with a group of adults who share a known preferred learning style—say, lecture with questions and answers—the best approach is to be as eclectic as possible so that most learners experience at least some exposure to their preferred learning style. In general, it is advisable to be more conservative and customary at the outset, prior to asking learners to engage in something that is less familiar, such as role-play or a simulation game. Show respect for learners who could possibly feel threatened by group process techniques by introducing them gradually and with adequate explanation as to why they are being used.

Too often, well-intentioned adult educators put learners through unfamiliar learning techniques without first explaining their benefits. This can make the learners feel both manipulated and confused as to why they are being asked to do certain things. And when this happens, learning is adversely affected.

As we shall see in the final chapter, not all learning techniques are equally suited for accomplishing certain learning objectives. So the adult catechetical leader will not only have to choose the right technique, but also help the learners "learn how to learn" using that technique. We will say more about this a little later in this chapter.

AS ADULTS GROW IN RESPONSIBILITY, EXPERIENCE, AND CONFIDENCE, SELF-CONCEPT MOVES FROM DEPENDENCY TO INDEPENDENCY

In his book, *The Modern Practice of Adult Education*, Malcolm Knowles presents the self-concept of adults as perhaps the most significant factor differentiating the learning theory and practice of adults from that of children.[49] Children are dependent upon adults in many ways, including what it is that they will learn. By contrast, adults are self-directed and totally free to decide if, what, and when they will learn. This, says Knowles, makes all the difference in how you approach the continuing education of adults.

For starters, you cannot, under normal circumstances, force adults to participate in learning programs. Rather, you must attract them to what is being offered because the topic speaks to their interests or, more compellingly, to their needs. This is why experienced adult educators put so much emphasis on discerning the learning interests and needs of the adult population they are serving, or, better yet, helping them discern their own needs. We will discuss techniques for doing this in the chapter on program planning.

Some directors of religious education (DREs) compel parents to attend first sacraments preparation programs with threats that their children will not receive the sacrament if they do not comply. The intentions of these catechetical leaders are understandable. They do not want children to receive first sacraments unless their parents are prepared to support them both in the preparation process as well as in living the sacramental life. Without parental involvement, the children's continued sacramental participation is threatened. But in approaching parents this way, there is a serious risk involved.

The risk is that parents are put in a "do it or else" situation, which only serves to undercut their self-image as mature adults who are quite capable of deciding what is in the best interests of their children. DREs inclined to use such tactics would be better served by putting the emphasis on winning the parents' cooperation through well-formulated explanations as to why their involvement is so crucial to the faith life of their children.

A second point about adults being self-directed is that the entire pastoral approach to them should be one that recognizes and respects their stature as mature individuals. An authoritarian approach to ministry that underscores obligation rather than spiritual opportunity only serves to dissuade adults from participating in any educational offerings of the parish. As noted in the first chapter, today's adults are making up their own minds about church affiliation, and every effort must be made to approach them with all due regard and respect for the status in life they have achieved.

A third implication flowing from adults' self-concept is that they are accustomed to influencing their environment, the things that impact their lives. This means that adults can play a significant role in helping shape various aspects of the learning process, from the topics chosen, to the design used, to the kind of follow-up desired. Once adults have participated in a program such as one on the first sacraments, there is no reason that their ideas for improving the program cannot be tapped and that they cannot be used as resource persons. This respects their experience and their ability to make a difference in designing and presenting the program.

Finally, adults expect to be taken seriously as learners and valued as unique individuals who have something to

offer. The learning atmosphere should therefore be welcoming, friendly, and informal, in which each adult is known by name. Think of treating adults in a learning situation as you would treat them as guests in your home. You would make sure that they are comfortable and that their needs are attended to. Adult catechetical situations are no different. The same respect and sensitivity should be shown to adults in the classroom as in a living room.

THE LEARNER'S EXPERIENCE IS A MAJOR RESOURCE IN LEARNING SITUATIONS

As has been previously noted, adults, almost by definition, bring a great deal of experience to learning situations. This has several implications for the adult catechetical leader.

First, it is imperative that whatever experience adults have on a topic be utilized as a rich resource for all the learners. Take, for example, prayer. You can bring in an expert in Catholic spirituality to talk about prayer and its various forms. If the speaker is good, the participants will undoubtedly give the experience favorable reviews. But in this example, only the experience of the speaker was drawn upon, while the literally hundreds of collective years of experience of the learners trying their best to pray were left untapped.

There is a lot of wisdom in that room that would go untapped unless the speaker had the wisdom to build into the learning process the learners' insights, their wisdom gained from trial and error along the spiritual journey. In many learning situations, the experience of the learners is the most valuable resource present, and it should be utilized to the fullest extent possible.

Second, many adult Catholics, especially those born before Vatican II, have low regard for their own experience when it comes to matters of theology or, for that matter, of faith. They tend to rely on authorities to give definitive information about most matters rather than trust their own insights. A major problem with this is that such individuals lose out on learning from their own experience. The adult catechetical leader should help such individuals to value their own experience and insights more as touch points of grace in their lives. Asking such questions as "What has your experience taught you about this issue?" not only helps them reflect on their experience but also helps them see the value that you, the catechetical leader, put on their experience. One of the essential tasks of adult educators is to help learners reflect upon and derive meaning from their experiences.

Third, while experience is an invaluable resource in the learning process, it can also be a hurdle to overcome. Not all experiences will help facilitate one's taking in of new information. If the information runs contrary to one's experience, then additional time and care will be needed for the teacher and learner to work through the clash between past experience and new ideas.

Finally, it is important to note that in most learning situations experience is the trump card. If you are speaking from theory, however well-founded it may be, and it runs contrary to people's experience, they will rely on their experience rather than on what you are presenting. It doesn't mean that either your facts or their experience is wrong; rather it is to suggest that truth can be multi-faceted and lends itself to multiple perspectives.

I had experienced this while serving as a volunteer on a task force dealing with an aspect of health care services. Since I did not know much about the field, I read a lot of research on the topic. Later, at one meeting, in response to a question put to the task force, I shared what I knew from reading the literature. When I finished, a women with great experience in directing a health care facility began by saying, "That is interesting information, but it is not my experience." She went on in detail explaining her experience, citing example after example. I could add nothing more since my knowledge was strictly "head" knowledge. She had what really mattered, and her views made the difference in how the task force proceeded.

It is often easy for those of us well-versed in theology to speak fluidly and convincingly from what we have read rather than from what we have personally experienced. That happens a lot to anyone in education or ministry. But we must be cautious to surface what experience is in the room on the topic so that we can gain as complete a picture of the truth as possible.

In this regard, keep in mind that people's perceptions and experience of the same issue can lead to a variety of insights and dispositions. This is all the more reason to get as many learners as possible to add their experience and insights to the discussion. There is, as former Harvard social psychologist Gordon Allport noted, virtually no possibility for any one formulation to capture the completeness or precise emphasis of a religious disposition as it exists in any single mature adult.[50] One of the goals of adult catechesis is to help believers understand and appreciate the multifaceted nature of religious truth. Not everything can be easily formulated in doctrinal statements.

ADULTS TEND TO BE LIFE-CENTERED IN THEIR ORIENTATION TOWARD LEARNING

In my early years as a parish adult catechetical leader, I often facilitated one of the adult learning groups that met on a regular basis. On one of those occasions, the group I was leading wanted to focus on Christology. I provided the reading material and led the discussions each week. As the topic drew to a close, I was pleased with how the discussions had gone and the benefits I perceived the learners were getting from them. But at the conclusion of the final session, one of the group members, a lawyer, said, "Neil, this has been very interesting, and I have learned a lot. But what I didn't find in our discussions was how all this applies to my work as a lawyer." I was stunned into silence and realized that my whole emphasis had been on the theology of Christ, but a theology devoid of any practical applications for the learners.

That was an important lesson for me, and it was one that was reinforced time and again as I pursued a graduate degree in adult education. Adult learners are very practically oriented when it comes to their continuing education. And most of what they want to learn stems from the life-transition issues that they are dealing with, such as finding a job, getting married or divorced, having a baby, learning a new skill to advance on the job, gaining parenting skills, and so on.

Research shows that, among adults engaged in learning, 83 percent do so because of life changes and 56 percent are drawn to topics related to career. Another 16 percent study family issues, while 13 percent focus on leisure. Then there is a significant falling off of percentages, to where art, health, and religion garner 5 percent, 5 percent, and 4 percent, respectively, of the adult learners. Issues of citizenship attract only 1 percent of the adult learning population.[51]

These statistics should come as no surprise to any experienced adult catechetical leader who has struggled to attract learners to various offerings. With rare exceptions, the same people seem to show up for the programs, regardless of what the topic is. They are like the 17 percent of adults who learn for the sake of the learning experience; for them, learning is its own justification. But for 83 percent of the adult population, learning is utilitarian, intended to provide some benefit, some better way of dealing with the life issues confronting them every day.

Obviously, there is not a sharp demarcation between those two categories of learners. The reasons adults engage in continuing education are often mixed. But, generally, most adult Catholics see the menu of topics offered in a parish as interesting, perhaps even beneficial to attend if they had the time, but hardly necessary for their spiritual well-being. For the moment, they have more important matters to attend to, such as trying to make ends meet this month; taking care of the multiple, complex needs of children; or figuring out what to do with a parent struggling with dementia.

Adult catechetical leaders would be better served if they took up some of the issues that are occupying the minds of their adult parishioners and explore them under the light of the Gospel on those topics. There is virtually nothing that is going on in the lives of adults, whether it is home life, work, or social issues, that does not have religious and spiritual significance. The challenge is to help adults experience what matters most in their lives in terms of Gospel values.

This is not to dismiss the need for courses, lectures, and seminars on topics ranging from Christ to sacraments to the Church. Rather, it is to suggest that most people are concerned with life-transition issues, and Christ, sacraments, and Church can and should be examined in relation to those issues. That is where they will have their most meaning and impact on the learners.

Look at it this way. You can offer a course on the Bible, working your way through the books. Or, you can offer a course, say, on the meaning of suffering in life and use the Book of Job and other books of the Bible to illuminate that topic. Which course will attract the most attendees? I think the answer is obvious. The former is a kind of theoretical treatment of scripture. The latter is an exploration of what most adults experience, struggle with, and try to make sense of. In both approaches, people are learning the scriptures.

ADULTS ARE MOTIVATED TO LEARN BY A VARIETY OF FACTORS

There is probably no more frequently asked question of trainers in adult religious education than "How do I motivate people to turn out for our programs?" As I noted earlier, the percentage of parishioners attending most parish-based adult catechetical programs is abysmally low—certainly in the single digits.

Fortunately, parish-based adult catechetical programs do not represent the complete picture of faith learning by Catholic adults. Besides the instruction they receive at liturgy, many Catholics are involved in a variety of movements such as Renew, Christ Renews His Parish, Marriage Encounter, and Cursillo. They also attend retreats and expand their knowledge through reading diocesan and national newspapers, Catholic magazines, books, and Web sites and by watching cable television. There are also the courses and seminars offered by Catholic colleges and universities.

Still, parish programs have the advantage of being both easily available to large numbers of Catholics and, if designed properly, a way of engaging them in a more systematic exploration of the faith. So, the question of how to attract adult parishioners to parish programs is a crucial question for pastors and adult catechetical leaders.

I will address the issue of specific strategies and techniques for motivating adults to attend programs in the chapter on program planning. For now, suffice it to say that motivating adults is more of a shotgun approach than it is a single bullet strategy. (Please forgive my gun metaphor.) There is no one factor that influences adults to attend continuing education programs, especially when it comes to religion. Everything from topic selection, to the timing of the program, to whether or not there are childcare provisions, to one's attitudes about the parish impact the decision to attend a program or not.

At this point, I want to make just two general observations about motivating influences. The first, as has already been noted, is that people are deeply influenced by the parish culture. Parishes that are vibrant, engaged in lots of ministerial outreach, and place a priority on adult faith formation will have an easier time of attracting adults to its programs.

Some years back when I was the representative for adult education at the United States Conference of Catholic Bishops, I was invited to conduct a day of training on adult faith formation for pastors and priests in a Midwest diocese. At the conclusion, the Midwest pastor I referred to in the chapter on parish approached me with this story of his own efforts at attracting parishioners to his adult education programs:

> We tried everything, but people just didn't turn out. Finally, we decided to turn our attention to social outreach. First, we identified lots of things that we felt needed addressing in the community, such as collecting food for the local homeless shelters, visiting people in our hospitals and prisons, and working on affordable housing. Then we invited parishioners to volunteer for these ministries. Lots of folks stepped forward, which delighted us. After a while, those same people started to ask for adult faith formation programs to address some of the questions that were starting to surface as they went about their ministries. It was the actual living out of their Christian vocation that sparked their interest in knowing more about their faith.

His comments made me think of that old adage: "It is easier to act your way into a new way of thinking (believing) than it is to think your way into a new way of acting." If we want people to take an interest in learning more about their faith, give them opportunities to make their faith more active, especially on behalf of others. It is my experience that people are generally more willing to give time and effort to help address a need than they are to spend time in a religious education classroom. Action can be a powerful motivator to learning.

Finally, don't disregard the importance of leadership style in motivating people to learn more about their faith. If there is no "juice," no charisma, no compelling energy coming from the parish leadership, there is a significant gap for drawing people to adult education programs. Like it or not, we are all influenced by our leaders. Those who inspire us frequently gain our support and involvement. If Jesus didn't have appeal as a leader and teacher, he would not have attracted disciples. People wanted to hear him and ultimately follow him because they were drawn to his vision, his commitment, and his passion for doing God's will. Parish leadership that is more attuned to organizational maintenance than it is to stirring parishioners' imaginations to the possibilities of living the Gospel at this time and in this place are themselves unwitting deterrents to people's interest in learning more about their faith.

ACTIVE LEARNER PARTICIPATION IN THE LEARNING PROCESS CONTRIBUTES TO LEARNING

This principle of active learner participation is one that holds throughout the lifespan when it comes to learning effectiveness. Teachers of all ages of students have long known that the more engaged they can help the students become in the learning process, the more effective the learning. "Don't just tell them; show them," and "Don't just show them; have them discover it for themselves" are mantras in contemporary education.

We tend to forget this when it comes to adult education because we think that adults, by virtue of their maturity, don't have to be "occupied" for good learning to take place. After all, they are not going to fidget or throw spitballs. They can actively listen, take notes if they want to, and draw their own conclusions. But when we fail to give them the opportunity to tap into their own experience and enrich the process of that experience through discussion and other activities, we shortchange their learning potential. Besides, adults have the wisdom, the experience, and the ability in many situations to serve actively as co-presenters, such as when invited to serve on a reaction panel to a formal presentation or to be group leaders.

At the same time, as I previously mentioned, not all learners like to learn the same way. And it is wise to go easy at first in asking adults to engage in a lot of action-oriented activities. Some might feel threatened by such activities until they feel more secure in the learning environment. Still others, whose preferred learning styles are more "heady," might prefer to sit and listen quietly to a speaker. And let's be honest—it is a little harder for adults to get up and move around, and their resistance to do so shows at times. We've all heard the groan and seen the eyes roll when a facilitator asks a group of adults to get into small groups.

There is a takeoff on the Matthew account of the last judgment that has a bit of truth in it about this very point. In the account, God gathers everyone to learn of their final fate. To the good, God says, "Enter into the kingdom of heaven where you will be eternally happy." To the bad, God says, "For your punishment, you must break into small groups forever."

It is good to help adults gradually become more comfortable with a variety of learning activities, a topic I will address more fully below. Gaining wisdom in the spiritual life through the pursuit of knowledge is not something that can come through only one approach to learning. A variety of methods are important to help adults experience and better understand various aspects of discipleship.

A COMFORTABLE, SUPPORTIVE ENVIRONMENT IS KEY TO SUCCESSFUL LEARNING

As I have mentioned several times, adults are loath to put themselves in any situation where they could possibly feel embarrassed, deficient, or otherwise threatened. And since they can choose to attend or not, the adult catechetical leader has to do everything possible to ensure that prospective learners will both anticipate and experience a comfortable, supportive environment.

When it comes to perception, a parish that exudes warmth, hospitality, and friendliness will have an easier time attracting parishioners to its programs. And that removes one more motivational hurdle.

Adult catechetical leaders should strive to have their programs be welcoming, supportive experiences for the attendees. For example, rather than simply allowing attendees to enter the room and find their way to a seat, the facilitator or host can greet them at the door and help connect them with other learners—much as he or she would do if people were arriving at their home for a party.

That same tone needs to carry over into the learning activities. Expressions of welcome and other acts of hospitality will help participants feel good about coming and more disposed to engage in the learning process. More importantly, it will help them relax, which is an important prerequisite for effective learning. Few of us do well in a learning situation when we are uptight about something. We will risk less, holding back rather than asking to be recognized to clarify a question we have. Anxiety or discomfort is a learning dampener.

When learners make a comment or raise a question, it is always good practice to thank them for their contribution. All of us like to feel that a comment we made or a question we posed added something worthwhile to the discussion. So, affirming these learning interventions not only helps boost learner self-confidence but also contributes to the relaxed and welcoming tone that you want to establish for the learning environment.

Finally, make sure that the entire physical environment is adult-friendly, from the chairs, lighting, and acoustics to climate control. The aroma of freshly brewed coffee, along with something tasty to snack on, will also do wonders for helping participants feel good about how seriously you are keeping their comfort in mind.

As a parish catechetical leader, I used to take great care to arrange a room to suit the needs of a particular learning experience. For example, if the program were going to invite participants to share elements of their personal faith journeys, I would bring in floor and table lamps so that I could turn off the harshly bright overhead florescent lights. The more subdued and warm light tone changed the room's ambiance to one that was more conducive for participants to speak about aspects of their faith life. You could even hear the difference in their softer voice tones as they spoke to each other in their groups.

Many Protestant parishes that put a high priority on adult faith formation have specially dedicated rooms that are furnished appropriately for adults. The existence of these rooms helps boost the parish's efforts to let congregants know that lifelong learning and discipleship go hand in hand.

ADULT LEARNERS BENEFIT FROM LEARNING HOW TO LEARN

One year when I was a parish catechetical leader, I decided to offer a program on spirituality called *Genesis II*. It had been designed by Trappist Father Vincent Dwyer and was receiving highly favorable reviews. The program used a combination of film and print resources and employed a variety of learning methodologies, such as small group discussion, faith sharing, and ritual gestures.

A good number of people signed up to take the course. One of them was Ella, a woman I knew well who had emigrated from Scotland. On the opening night, Ella told me that she had longed to delve deeper into spirituality and was very excited to be part of this course. To my surprise, only two sessions later she informed me that she was withdrawing from the course. When I asked why, she simply said that the program wasn't what she had hoped it would be.

I came to later realize, knowing Ella as I did, that the program was in fact something that she could have benefited from. But I had failed her by not preparing her and the other learners to understand how to get the most out of the learning methodologies that the program used. As a learner, Ella was a quiet observer and listener, possibly a result of her having a heavy accent. In any case, when unfamiliar, action-oriented activities were introduced, she became uncomfortable and concluded that the program was not for her.

Some months later, I used the course again on a retreat for single adults. Only this time I learned from my mistake and took care to explain the purpose and function of each learning methodology and how to get the most from them. The program was a great success.

An adult catechetical leader's responsibility for programming includes not only making sure that the offerings are well designed and effectively implemented, but also ensuring that the learners get the most out of them. This often means helping the participants learn how to learn effectively from the methodologies that are going to be used.

This wouldn't be so much an issue if faith learning were exclusively a matter of absorbing information and drawing conclusions. We are all familiar with that. A speaker presents something, some questions are asked, and discussion takes place. It is all very discursive and logical, the kind of learning we were subjected to throughout our schooling.

But when it comes to faith, we are not dealing exclusively with facts. We are delving into the realm of mystery, where insight is often better mediated through story, metaphor, ritual, and actions. This is why when we gather each Sunday as the community of believers, we engage in ritualistic acts that pull us deeply into the mystery of Christ's life, death, and resurrection. Indeed, the early fathers of the Church spoke of the illuminative powers of the sacraments, their ability to help us understand in ways that would not otherwise be possible.

A primary treasury of our faith is sacred scripture. Yet scripture is not a collection of doctrinal statements; it is a gathering of faith stories, stories that are told using a variety of literary forms. The power of story is that it is open-ended, lending itself to ever-deeper insight and meaning. The scriptures were the perfect way for the early Church to communicate the mystery of Jesus to those of us who followed centuries later.

As we shall see in the final chapter, different desired learning outcomes require different methodologies, some of which are aimed more at our hearts than our heads. These methodologies, however, need to be explained so that the learners can understand them and thereby get the most from them.

Some years ago, I was conducting a weeklong course in adult education as part of a non-traditional doctoral program. This particular program was located in San Francisco, and the learners were a combination of lay men and women, religious, and priests that came from communities surrounding the bay. As was my custom, I invited the students to volunteer to prepare and lead the opening prayer each morning. One of those volunteers asked if she could incorporate dance as part of the prayer service. I agreed.

When her turn came, she led us in song, a scripture reading, and some quiet time. Then she turned on some soft music and began to make slow, rhythmic movements. I could see immediately that she was interpreting the scripture passage that had been read, and I marveled at how she was able to bring additional meaning to it through her movements. As I looked around the room, I could see that the other learners were similarly absorbed in the experience. The prayer went on a little longer than I had planned, but it was a most unique and moving experience. But not everyone was similarly pleased.

When the prayer ended, a priest rushed up to me, his face flushed. "Look," he seethed, "I'm a busy pastor who just spent forty minutes in heavy traffic getting here. This so-called opening prayer took valuable time away from our getting on with the course. I don't have time for this nonsense."

As a man who spent at least four years studying theology in terms of doctrinal formulations, his reaction was understandable. I only wish that I had thought to better prepare the class for a prayer service that would include movement. At the same time, it was clear to me that for him, learning was about getting information, hearing what I had to say as the instructor. Something like movement was simply not a tool in his learning inventory.

In recent years, Harvard educator Howard Gardner has helped us understand that there are different kinds of intelligences besides those that relate primarily to absorbing information.[52] For example, his research identifies other intelligences like music, movement, and interpersonal activity. For people with such intelligences, understanding often comes best to them when their special giftedness is called upon.

Such a range of intelligences should not be overlooked as we seek to help contemporary believers probe deeper into their own spirituality and the divine mystery. Words, especially in the form of doctrine, will take us so far, but ultimately we will also need to draw upon other learning strategies. And when we do, we owe it to the learners to help them know how to get the most from them.

We can do no better than to take our lead from Jesus, the master teacher. He used a variety of learning strategies to reach his listeners, such as story, parable, gesture, metaphor, and yes, movement. Jesus understood that grasping religious truth is a matter of using both the head and the heart.

Finally, another aspect of helping adults learn how to learn is to help them plan for how they will put their learning into practice. People often fail to apply their learning simply because they didn't think through how to get started and stay the course. For example, someone might attend a workshop on program planning, but then never operationalize her insights because she didn't anticipate some of the implications of making the switch from her current way of planning.

Learning, moreover, isn't completed when the program ends; the program is only the beginning. Learning expands and deepens as we make efforts to apply it. When we fail to apply what we have learned, we cut off a major part of our learning potential.

We fail our learners when we do not build into our program ways for them to strategize about what happens after the program ends. We consider our job done when we have given them the information or skills identified in the objectives. But that is only part of our responsibility. We are also responsible for helping them learn how to continue building upon what they gained in the program.

Failures in this regard often happen with ministry development seminars or courses. The participants get excited about what they are learning, only later to discover that no one back at the parish or diocese shares their enthusiasm for making changes. As a result their excitement eventually peters out, along with their good insights. Had they been given an opportunity to strategize about how they might deal constructively with resistance to change, things might have turned out differently.

Consider the mother who completes a course on centering prayer and is serious about doing it on a daily basis. By providing her with opportunities to think through how she can apply her learning back home, you are helping her to ensure that her learning will take root and thrive. If, on the other hand, she is left to return home to face an already jammed family schedule with three small kids, a husband who works long hours, and her own part-time job, her best intentions may well become causalities of the clock.

By designing application strategies right into the learning process you are ensuring that this important step will not be overlooked. You are also able to utilize the learners, themselves, as important, if not essential, resources in the application process. When it comes to practical application, the learners are often the best resources for helping each other think through how best to get it done. By virtue of their practical wisdom and relevant experience, they are equipped to help each other's learnings become ongoing successes rather than flash-in-the-pan episodes.

Working successfully with adults as learners is primarily a matter of attending to and utilizing the maturity, wisdom, and experience that they have attained. It also means recognizing that they are quite capable of engaging in the discovery process themselves, and that the more they can direct their own learning, the better they will learn. This is especially true in the realm of faith, where the goal of learning is an ever-deepening conversion of the heart, mind, and will to be a more faithful disciple of Jesus Christ.

Questions for Reflection

1. What kind of learner do you consider yourself to be in terms of learning style preference? In other words, how do you best like to learn?

2. Have you discovered any differences in learning style preference among various ethnic populations? If so, what might those be?

3. What in your view is the most important thing that has to be kept in mind when working with adult learners?

4. What steps can be taken in your parish to help adults realize that discipleship means a commitment to lifelong learning in the faith?

5. What do you feel are the most pressing learning needs for Catholic adults today?

6. What can your parish do to create learning facilities that are more adult oriented?

7. What in your view is holding back some Catholic adults from being more interested in learning more about their faith?

CHAPTER 4

Attending to the Voice of God as Teacher

Adult catechesis is not exclusively about teachers, resources, and programming. The journey to mature Christian faith also involves substantial inner spiritual work by individuals. The task of adult catechetical leaders is to help those to whom they minister realize that God is always present to them as teacher—indeed, that God is their primary teacher. St. Augustine, in a dialogue with his son Adeodatus, refers to God as the interior teacher who gives us wisdom. And, in fact, he viewed God as the only teacher of the soul.[53]

Like all good teachers, however, God requires of learners a certain readiness to learn. And that is where dedication to the interior life becomes an important prerequisite. The Sufis, Islam's ancient mystical sect, have a saying about this: "He who knows himself, knows the Lord."

The renowned German Jesuit theologian Karl Rahner said that tomorrow's Christian will be a mystic or not at all. He was not suggesting that we all become monastic-type contemplatives. But he was saying that given the challenges of living in contemporary society, a strong contemplative attitude, the building of an interior life, would be needed to faithfully live one's Christian vocation. We are otherwise likely to be swept away from our religious moorings by the currents of worldly concerns.

Jesuit moral theologian Richard A. McCormick sees efforts to be enlightened by God's teachings as no easy task, however. "Our growing enlightenment is a fragile and vulnerable undertaking," he writes. "We resist it because it can be painful and demanding. Before we can deal with the forces of good and evil in ourselves, we must be able to recognize them."[54] He goes on to say that there are many forces that work against our self-discernment, which is the beginning of conversion. We resort to self-deception, rationalization, the comforts of complacency, and all kinds of denials and repressions. For this reason, he suggests that our daily prayer be, "Lord that I may see." Indeed, and to that I would add, "Lord that I may hear."

The struggle to see and to hear, to clear away our spiritual blindness and deafness, is essentially what it means to be contemplative, to be a mystic. Contemplation is simply quieting ourselves down, focusing on our inner lives so that we can more readily discern the subtle intonations of God's voice.

The scriptures are full of references to God as teacher. The psalmist prays, "Teach me to do your will, for you, O Lord, are my God" (Ps 143:10); "In the secret of my heart, teach me wisdom" (Ps 51:6). In Deuteronomy, Moses tells the Israelites that "[God's] word is very near to you, already in your mouths and in your hearts; you have only to carry it out" (Dt 30:14). Isaiah prophesies that "No longer will your Teacher [God] hide himself, but with your own eyes you shall see your Teacher, while from behind, a voice shall sound in your ears, 'This is the way; walk in it . . . '" (Is 30:20–21).

In the New Testament, Jesus tells Peter that it was God who taught him about the true nature of his messianic role (Mt 16:17). And Paul tells the Thessalonians, "God himself has taught you to love one another" (1 Thes 4:9). However, most important for us as Jesus' disciples is his assurance that he will send us the Spirit, who will guide us to the truth (Jn 16:13). The

Christian disciple is never without God's Spirit—teaching and guiding.

The Church reminds us of God's teaching voice each day in its Liturgy of the Hours. At the outset of Morning Prayer, Psalm 95 is recited. It contains the admonition, "Today, listen to the voice of the Lord." It is a beautiful way to remind ourselves at the start of each day of our contemplative calling. We are to dedicate ourselves to listening to God's voice—and, hopefully, to learning from it.

Contemplation or attuning ourselves to God's voice is a spiritual exercise that takes practice and dedication. While God has blessed us with innate longings that continually remind us of our divine destiny, the pressures and din of everyday life can make it difficult for us to hear and attend to God's voice. In order to overcome these hurdles, we need to take on spiritual practices, dispositions of the heart and mind, that will help us listen more closely to God's teachings. Among them is the cultivation of silence, detachment, humility, patience, and attentiveness.

These spiritual practices are ones that adult catechetical leaders should not only seek to inculcate in adult learners but also to make a virtue in their own lives. It is impossible to be a spiritual guide for others when we have not made the journey ourselves. With this in mind, let us now look at each of these five spiritual practices in turn.

1. Silence

In urban society today, silence is an endangered species. Our senses are constantly being engaged by ever-present noise and visual stimulation. As a result, we are becoming increasingly addicted to them. It is hard for many children to study without the television or radio on or for many teens and adults to drive without the car radio, CD player, or iPod switched on. Look around. You will see people everywhere talking on cell phones, checking e-mail on Blackberries, or texting. Even a brief ride up an elevator surrounds us with canned music. Increasingly we are becoming plugged in to and dependent upon electronic sights and sounds. We can literally occupy our days without hosting a single reflective thought.

On August 8, 2005, *Time* magazine ran a cover story about youngsters turning thirteen. On the cover was an adolescent girl posing before the camera with white iPod ear bud cords streaming down over her shoulders. Two years later in another cover story about national service, *Time* showed a young Rosie-the-Riveter-look-alike flexing her muscles. Again, white ear bud chords garnished her face. These devices have become so prevalent that *Time* obviously sees them as normal, if not necessary, accoutrements to a modern lifestyle.

Recently, I spotted our trash collector jump off the truck with a Bluetooth device on his ear. That is one of those gadgets that lets you talk on your cell phone without using your hands. I asked him about it, and he said, smiling, "Yeah, now I don't miss any calls; I'm always connected."

Always connected. Actually, that is not a bad metaphor for the mystical or contemplative state of which Rahner spoke. Rabbi Adin Steinsaltz, an Israeli-born scholar, emphasizes that God's voice is speaking all the time; our task is to listen. "God's voice doesn't stop," he says, "we just stop hearing." We need to stay connected to what God is teaching us with the same fervor that our culture seems to have us plugged into instant communications with one another.

Silence is a key means by which we are better able to stay connected to the divine teacher, although certainly it is not the only means. God speaks to us through our children and mates, through the poor and suffering, through Church teachings, scripture and liturgy, through world events and, yes, through the songs streaming through our iPods and the images filling our TVs. As Catholics, we believe that virtually all of existence is pregnant with God's presence. As Julian of Norwich expressed it, "The fullness of joy is to behold God in everything."

Still, silence has a special role to play in the life of the adult learner. God's voice is often subtle, barely discernable. One must quiet down and listen carefully, receptively. The psalmist reminds us, "Be still and know that I am God" (Ps 46:10).

One of my favorite scripture passages about the subtleness of God's voice is 1 Kings 19:11–13. In that passage, God tells the prophet Elijah to go stand on a mountain because the Lord will be passing by:

> A strong and heavy wind was rending the mountains and crushing rocks before the Lord—but the Lord was not in the wind. After the wind there was an earthquake—but the Lord was not in the earthquake.

> After the earthquake there was fire—but the Lord was not in the fire. After the fire, there was a tiny whispering sound.

> When he heard this, Elijah hid his face in his cloak and went and stood at the entrance of the cave. A voice said to him, "Elijah, why are you here?"

"Why are you here?" Isn't that a wonderful, contemplative question? Why am I here? What is God asking of me? What is the meaning of my life? What should I be doing to please God?

The purpose of practicing silence in our lives is so that we can clear our heads, calm our hearts, and listen attentively—expectantly—for God to speak to us about those kinds of questions. And that is what God, our teacher, wants to do. But like Elijah, we need to look past much of the sound and fury going on around us so that we can better focus on the tiny whispering sound of God's voice—not outside us, but deep within us.

Herman Melville, author of *Moby Dick* and other literary masterpieces, said, "All profound things and emotions of things are preceded and attended by silence. Silence is the general consecration of the universe. Silence is the laying on of the Divine Pontiff's hands upon the world. Silence is the only voice of our God."[55]

He was not alone in his eulogizing of the power of silence. Thomas Merton, a Trappist monk whose life was contextualized by silence, said, "A person who loves God necessarily loves silence." And Meister Eckhart, the fourteenth-century monk and mystic, said, "There is nothing so much like God as silence."[56]

In the Quaker tradition, silence is the primary mediator of God's presence and guidance. They believe that one connects with the divine directly with no need for mediation by other people or rituals. They gather for community worship and sit in silence, listening for God's voice in their individual hearts and attentively waiting for the Spirit to move someone in the assembly to speak aloud. Learning from God is both a private and public matter, with silence as the common ingredient.

Archbishop of Canterbury Rowan Williams says that if there is one virtue that was almost universally recommended by the desert fathers and mothers, it is silence. They did so, he says, because without silence we cannot get closer to knowing who we are before God.

"Silence is letting what there is be what it is," says Williams. "In that sense it has to do profoundly with God: the silence of simply being. We experience that at times when there is nothing we can say or do that would not intrude on the integrity and the beauty of that being."[57] This is why, I am convinced, we as humans dedicate a moment of silence, such as at a public event, when some tragedy has occurred. We cannot come up with a deeper way of honoring the memory of what took place than to stand together in silence. Silence is our highest tribute.

Silence can take a myriad of forms, from classic meditative practices to simple activities that we find conducive to focusing our thoughts. St. John of the Cross said that God calls us by putting desire within us. Some of the things that we find most enjoyable can at the same time be a source of quiet solitude in which we become disposed to hearing God's voice. After an intense week at work, my wife likes to retreat for a spell to a favorite soft chair, light a candle, and read the scriptures or spiritual books. For others it might be the easy pace of fishing on a lake. For still others it might be crocheting, needlepoint, gardening, bird-watching, or a quiet walk. The point is to bring some degree of solitude and silence into our lives so that we are more openly receptive to perceiving God's gentle nudgings. Deep within we long to be attentive to the master teacher.

2. Detachment

As Catholics we have all been taught the dangers of becoming too attached to things. Attachment compromises our ability to make the right choices, just as it did for the rich young man whom Jesus admired. We read in the gospels that Jesus was very impressed with a young man's dedication to keeping the commandments and invited him to become one of his disciples, after he disposed of his possessions. But the young man went away sad because he had so many things that he would have had to give up if he followed Jesus (Mt 19:16–30; Mk 10:17–31; Lk 18:18–30).

The gospels are filled with warnings about the seductive power of attachment to things. Jesus likens attachment to serving two masters, eventually loving one and despising the other (Mt 6:24). On another occasion, he talks about how it would be easier for a camel to get through the eye of a needle than it would be for someone who is rich to enter the kingdom of heaven (Mt 19:24; Mk 10:25; Lk 18:25).

There is nothing wrong with having things and enjoying them. The problem arises when we allow them to dominate our consciousness and color our perspectives. Other concerns that should command our attention, such as helping those in need, get shoved aside or put on hold. Attachment is not so much a matter of what we own as it is a matter of what we allow to own us.

It would be difficult to overstate how strongly Jesus felt about this point. We cannot enter the kingdom of heaven, that is to say, live in accordance with God's will here and now, unless we have the right spirit, the right frame of mind. The behaviors of kingdom living, as Jesus describes in the Beatitudes, in the Final Judgment narrative in Matthew 25, and elsewhere, require that we be free to do what is right. That is why he blesses the "poor in spirit" because they are unhampered by concerns over possessions and better able to go beyond themselves to be peacemakers who are merciful and clean of heart (Mt 5:3–10).

What does this have to with learning? Everything. Our ability to take in new information, to objectively look at ourselves as spiritual pilgrims, to perhaps jettison wrong notions about our faith is dependent upon our being detached. As French author Simone Weil wrote in *Gravity and Grace,* "Attachment is the great fabricator of illusion; reality can only be obtained by someone who is detached." Attachment, whether to things or ideas, makes us see things the way we want to see them rather than how we need to see them.

We will not be able to discern God's voice if our attachments filter it out before we can even hear it. Jesus frequently railed against the self-imposed blindness and deafness of some of his hearers. They could not fathom what he was saying because they were so attached to their current way of understanding God, especially as it took shape through their interpretation of the Mosaic Law. For example, how could the vineyard owner give the same pay to those who worked one hour as he gave to those who worked all day? That's not how justice works according to the Law, right? And surely God would act not act contrary to the Law?

So it goes with us also. In order to hear God's voice in the silence of our hearts or in the events of our lives, we have to be open, expectantly receptive to the divine message, which can come at times from the most surprising sources. We can't do this, however, if our minds are closed down with prejudices and presumptions. Indeed, St. Thomas Aquinas said that presumption is the mother of error. We will see and hear what we expect to see and hear. And that is our loss as learners.

One of my favorite authors, Anne Morrow Lindberg, in her little jewel of a book, *Gift from the Sea*, wrote this about the danger of attachment in the form of false assumptions:

> Because of the false assumption that middle age is a period of decline, one interprets these life-signs, paradoxically, as signs of approaching death. Instead of facing them, one runs away; one escapes—into depression, nervous breakdown, drink, love affairs, or frantic, thoughtless, fruitless overwork. Anything, rather than face them. Anything, rather than stand still and learn from them. One tries to cure the signs of growth, to exorcise them as if they were devils, when really they might be angels of annunciation.[58]

"Angels of annunciation" is what so many happenings in our lives are. They are messages from God that call for our attention, if we are wise enough and open enough to see or hear them. But when we predetermine what is possible because of strongly held beliefs or attachments of any kind, we foreclose on any of these messages getting through.

Years ago when I was working with a group of single adults, they expressed an interest in hearing from some thoughtful atheists. They wanted to get a sense of why such people believed the way they did. So we invited representatives from the local ethical society to join us for an evening of discussion. One of them was a young man who spoke inspirationally of his conviction that, although he did not believe in a God, he felt ethically bound to do whatever was needed to alleviate suffering in the human family.

His companion was a young woman, who we quickly learned was a former Catholic. Her presentation focused on her rejection of Catholicism because of what she saw as absurd notions of God as a harsh judge who would often rain down severe punishments on his own children. She said that she simply could not believe in such a God.

When she finished, one of the participants rose and said that neither could she believe in such a God. She then described her understanding of God, especially in terms of God's loving embrace of the human family through Jesus. But the ethicist would hear none of it. She kept returning to the harsh notion of God and how impossible it was for her to believe in such a being. It became clear to the group as the discussion unfolded that despite attempts to help dispel the speaker's notions of Catholicism believing in a vengeful God, she could not hear what was being said to her. Her reasons for leaving the Church formed the foundation for how she now saw herself in the world. And her attachment to them trumped all voices to the contrary.

Adult catechetical leaders should help believers understand that attachments are potential blocks to learning. Hearing God's voice requires a degree of suppleness of mind and heart that leaves us open to overriding even long-held convictions. Certainly, mature faith involves strong commitment to beliefs. But that commitment is necessarily tempered with an openness to change graced by new insight.

3. Humility

Humility, as the Sufis speak of it, is not simply a virtue; it is a necessity for learning. Attachment locks us in place, blocking out the "angels of annunciation" God sends us. Humility, on the other hand, frees us to learn from everything and everybody. Pride can get in the way of our learning by circumscribing in advance who is acceptable for us to learn from or what is acceptable to learn. Humility, said St. Augustine, above all other virtues is the way that God communicates with us.[59]

We don't know how, when, or under what circumstances God will teach us. But we do know that if our pride decides in advance how God will not teach us, we become spiritually deaf. If we think it improbable, for example, that God could teach us anything through someone of a different race or culture, of less education, homeless, with an intellectual disability, or having different political or religious views, we will learn nothing. As God did with Elijah, God decides how God's voice will come to us. Humility enables us to stand like Elijah before the cave, open and waiting.

When it comes to being a learner in the faith, it helps to cultivate a personal theology of incompleteness. We don't have all the answers; we are not pinnacles of wisdom. We are an unfolding mystery, even to ourselves. We need to recognize our dependence upon others as sources of wisdom and truth. Each and every person can be an angel of annunciation to us, if we but have the wisdom and humility to see him or her as such.

One of my sisters used to have a sign posted on the wall of her teenage daughter's room that read: "Please be patient. God isn't finished with me yet." It served as a daily reminder to her that this particular child was a work in progress and that as a mother she needed to be patient and understanding, especially through the difficult years of adolescence. We would do well as learners to see ourselves as works in progress, hungry to learn whatever we can from whomever we can so we can grow in wisdom. And a little patience with ourselves wouldn't hurt, either.

Some years ago, I read an interview with a diocesan bishop in the daily newspaper. According to the article, the bishop said that he reads a book until he disagrees with something. He then puts the book away, having no further regard for the author's ideas. I couldn't help but contrast that with a friend of mine who at the time held a high position in the office of the U.S. Attorney General. He told me that he never picked up a book, even by someone with whom he frequently disagreed, without telling himself that there is something he can learn from it. With this outlook, he said, he was never been disappointed in what he discovered.

Two mindsets, two approaches to learning. One felt that his beliefs were correct and he could learn from others to the degree that they could enhance his current understanding or deepen the convictions he already held. The other felt that even disagreements, if broached honestly and humbly, could still be rich yeast for learning. It is all about having the humility to acknowledge that one can learn from anybody. As artist and writer James Prosek noted, "Humility is a big part of being open and receptive to everything you see. Part of being a good observer is to know you don't know anything."

Humility of this nature is not readily cultivated in our society today. Instead, everything in the public realm seems to be going in the direction of "I'm right and you're wrong." Political commentary TV shows, for example, have become panels of competing certitude, neither political party willing to admit that the other has anything of value to say. Religious rhetoric, too, has gotten sharper and more divisive over such emotionally charged issues as capital punishment, immigration, abortion, and stem cell research. Many have lost a comfort with or even a capacity to find common ground upon which to have an honest conversation or debate. They fear that doing so will somehow compromise the truth. But perhaps genuine learning can take place only when we listen to both those who agree with us as well as those who do not. Aquinas, a great teacher of the Church, believed that truth rested on examining diverse opinions. "We must love them both, those whose opinions we share and those whose opinions we reject," he said. "For both have labored in the search for truth and both have helped in finding it."[60] This is the kind of humility we need to cultivate in ourselves if we are to be effective listeners of God's voice.

4. Patience

A friend of mine who hosted an Arab exchange student for the better part of a year told me that what struck her guest most about our culture was our impatience. He observed that we Americans want things resolved virtually overnight, while in his country, Saudi Arabia, issues may take years to work through—and no one thinks the worse for it.

That sweeping characterization of us is not easily dismissed. We have grown accustomed to getting what we want when we want it. Want that new dress tomorrow? They can ship it overnight. Crazy about the new song you just heard? You can download it immediately. Need to know more about the new school principal? Just Google her. So much is readily available to us that patience in the face of delay is likely harder and harder for us to bear as individuals and as a society.

But patience is an essential component of the spiritual life, especially in terms of God teaching us. We are on God's schedule, not ours. "My thoughts are not your thoughts, nor are your ways my ways, says the Lord" (Is 55:8). Learning from God is not within our control. God teaches us how and when God chooses to do so. And more often than not, patience is a requirement of the divine pedagogy.

Part three of the *General Directory for Catechesis* (*GDC*) is entitled, "The Pedagogy of the Faith." Chapter 1 of that section begins with a description of the "pedagogy of God"—namely, how God has taught us down through time. According to the *GDC*, "[God] causes the person to grow progressively and patiently towards the maturity of a free son [or daughter], faithful and obedient to his word. To this end, as a creative and insightful teacher, God transforms events in the life of his people into lessons of wisdom."[61]

It is important to note that God's teaching process is about *progressive* and *patient* growth, not overnight success. It is also about transforming the events of our lives into *lessons of wisdom*. There is a direct correlation between our having patience and our gaining wisdom from the events around us. Without patience, we lose perspective on what is happening in the here and now. We lose touch with our innermost selves, with what is stirring within us. Impatience—and I know this firsthand—takes us outside of ourselves. Wherever we are, we are not where we should be. We are not focused on the current moment of revelation, on receiving whatever angels of annunciation God is sending our way.

A couple of years ago, I was driving home from work on a beautiful spring afternoon when I encountered a major traffic backup. Everything came to a total standstill. As I sat in the car trying to keep my frustration in check, I eyed the driver behind me in my rearview mirror. He flew into a rage. His face grew red and contorted; his mouth moved rapidly in what I assumed was a string of profanities. He began pounding on his steering wheel and then he seized the visor above his head with both hands and began to wrench it. His body shook with fury. I grew alarmed that he might suddenly smash into my car, but I could stand the sight no longer and turned away.

Within moments I found myself gazing at the mall that runs from the Capitol to the Lincoln Memorial spread out to my left. It was beautifully adorned with spring flowers, and the trees lining it were flush with deep green leaves shimmering in the warm sun. It was breathtaking. Just ahead in view was the Vietnam Memorial, with its wall of 60,000 names, a few of whom I knew. The juxtaposition of natural beauty and human tragedy struck me as odd, yet ripe with meaning.

I must have driven by this spot hundreds of times and not experienced what I did that day—all made possible by the stopped traffic. For those whose impatience got the better of them that day, an opportunity for possibly encountering a graced moment was lost. It's not that one had to take in the mall as I did. It could have come in the form of thoughts of family or friends or words coming from the radio. The point is that patience frees one to let God do the talking, from whatever the source.

Poet Rainer Maria Rilke offered the following advice to a young poet who was struggling with his craft:

I beg you ... to have patience with everything unresolved in your heart and try to love the questions themselves as if they were locked rooms or books written in a very foreign language. Don't search for the answers, which could not be given you now because you would not be able to live them. And the point is to live everything. Live the questions now. Perhaps, then, someday far in the future, you will gradually without ever noticing it, live your way into the answer.[62]

God often teaches in ways that require us to have a lot of patience. The lessons may not be in the answers but, as Rilke noted, in the questions themselves. The struggle with the questions is often where the grace is, where the possibilities for growth are. The desert fathers had a saying: "Go to your cell. It will teach you everything." In other words, wisdom and insight often come because we wrestle with the issue, not because we were provided an answer. Indeed, answers that are too quickly provided can often impede rather than aid spiritual learning.

Patience enables us to stay with the unresolved questions. Whether answers eventually come or not, the waiting and wondering are themselves avenues through which God may choose to teach us. As we read in the Letter to the Hebrews, God's promises are inherited through faith and patience (Heb 6:12, 14). There are no shortcuts in the pursuit of spiritual wisdom.

5. Attentiveness

As both the pace and complexity of modern life have increased, our personal and professional lives have accordingly become more pressurized and fragmented. In order to cope, we have had to make adjustments. We multitask. We learn to do a variety of things at the same time. It's the only way we seem to be able to stay afloat in the turbulent sea of demands on our attention. So we eat our lunch at our desk while pouring through the latest stack of reports. We talk on the phone to a colleague while continuing to type the memo that has to be on the boss's desk in an hour. We eat breakfast reading the newspaper, keeping an eye on the Weather Channel. We watch the evening news while conducting a conversation with our spouse or one of our kids. We talk to a friend on the phone while cooking dinner, washing the dishes, or driving the car.

The downside of trying to manage several things at the same time is that we cannot be fully present to any of them. And it is in being fully present to the moment that we can best discern what God may be saying to us—something perhaps we desperately need to hear.

Buddhist monk and author Thich Nhat Hanh has written extensively about the virtues of what he calls "mindfulness."[63] His advice is to give the present moment our full attention so that we can savor and learn from it. Through mindfulness, he says, we master and restore ourselves, and we enter fully into the world of reality, which itself is a miracle. This is something we Catholics should be very attuned to doing. We have a strong sense of sacramentality—that is, of seeing all creation as mediating God's presence. God is present in any given moment or situation, but it takes focus and attention to discern that presence and to learn from it.

Sometimes when I am speaking to someone on the phone, I hear the click-click of computer keys. During the conversation, the other person usually utters an "uh huh" from time to time to let me know that he or she is still on the line. But the keys keep moving, and I know that the listener's attention is partially elsewhere. Meanwhile, I wonder if he or she really hears what I am saying.

Picture this: A synagogue leader approaches Jesus about restoring his dead daughter to life (Mt 9:18–26). As he pleads his case, Jesus is listening and nodding to show that he hears him, but at the same time, he is checking his Blackberry for e-mail. We are horrified. The scene repulses us. It totally violates our sense of Jesus as Emmanuel, God *with* us.

Go ahead and choose any scene in the gospels where someone is talking to Jesus, and picture him multitasking, not giving that person his undivided attention. We can't imagine such a thing. Neither can we imagine that when we pray that God would somehow not be fully attending to our needs. Yet this is something that we have grown accustomed to doing ourselves. We excuse our actions by thinking that if we don't multitask, listening with one ear while also attending to something else, we will fall further behind. Or perhaps we feel that we are doing the person a favor by half listening since it is either that or not listening at all.

But when we fail to be fully present to someone who is speaking to us, we not only fail to fully respect that person but we also fail to enter into the moment as a potential encounter with God who teaches. Every human encounter is pregnant with possibilities of grace and revelation. But we must be fully attentive to discern them.

A few years ago, I was speaking with a colleague about a mutual friend who was dying of colon cancer. I inquired how our friend was dealing with his worsening situation. "He said that he just 'leans into the mystery' each day," was the reply. Those words have stayed with me, and I have thought about them often, both in terms of their meaning and of what they revealed about my friend's spiritual attitude in the face of death. Had I not been paying close attention to that conversation, I don't think I would have picked up on the special significance those words have since held for me.

Southern writer Eudora Welty said that long before she wrote stories, she would listen for stories. "Listening *for* them is something more acute than listening *to* them. I suppose it is an early form of participation in what goes on."[64] Listening *for* God is a spiritual disposition that we want to foster in ourselves as catechetical leaders and in adult learners. We want to listen for God's voice in our present circumstances, whatever they are. And we especially want to listen for God's voice coming from those we love, and with whom we live, work, and associate. We want to be attentive, watchful. God is teaching; we simply need to pay attention, listen, and learn.

Questions for Reflection

1. In what ways do you experience God as a teacher in your life?

2. Of the five suggested spiritual practices to attend to God as teacher, which ones hold the greatest promise for you?

3. What importance do you think the message of this chapter should be given within adult faith formation ministry?

4. What strategies might work best for helping adults to attend to God as their primary teacher?

5. What steps can you take to include a role for "God as Teacher" in your current programming?

CHAPTER 5

Supporting the Independent Learner

There are several reasons why today's adult catechetical leader needs to put more emphasis on supporting independent, self-directed learning. Briefly stated, they are:

1. Declining church attendance translates to low learning attendance.

2. The rising busyness of modern adult life limits time for ongoing education.

3. American religious individualism fosters self-directed spiritual seekers.

4. The Internet is changing the educational paradigm.

5. Mission warrants a rethinking of approaches to adult faith formation.

6. Self-discovery is at the heart of spiritual learning.

I will examine these reasons in some detail, arguing for parishes to commit more energy and resources toward supporting independent/self-directed learning. Then I will offer some practical guidance for developing a more robust outreach to independent learners.

Why Support Independent Learning?

DECLINING CHURCH ATTENDANCE TRANSLATES TO LOW LEARNING ATTENDANCE

No one who is familiar with modern parish life would disagree that attendance at adult education programs is abysmally low across the board. The problem is that, given current statistics about generational differences, we can presume that matters are only going to get worse. If fewer Catholics attend Mass, fewer of them will be available to take advantage of ongoing faith formation opportunities.

The 2005 survey of U.S. Catholics cited in chapter 1 showed a steady decline in church attendance from older to younger generations. Sixty percent of those sixty-five and older attended Mass weekly or more. Catholics who were between eighteen and twenty-five had an alarmingly poor attendance rate of only 15 percent. Even accounting for younger Catholic adults returning to church once they settle down, the outlook is not good. While overall church attendance has remained relatively steady for the past five years, strikingly different attitudes about church attendance by the youngest generations do not bode well for future liturgical participation.

Adult catechetical leaders will need to provide independent learning opportunities if they are to have any hope of reaching those who do not regularly attend church. If non-attendees can be reached at all, it will be easier to reach them where they are rather than to attract them to go where they usually do not. Admittedly, attracting non-churchgoers to a church-related educational program, even a self-directed one, is a challenge. But sometimes people's intellectual curiosity about matters spiritual is stronger than their willingness to sit through Mass. Independent learning provides a different way of reaching those who tend to stay at arm's length from institutional religion.

THE RISING BUSYNESS OF MODERN ADULT LIFE LIMITS TIME FOR ONGOING EDUCATION

Even for those Catholics who attend church regularly, the demands of modern life are increasingly squeezing their available time to participate in a parish program. For the average family, there are the countless things that have to be done for the kids, ranging from soccer practice to homework to SAT exams. Then there is the possibility that both parents have to work to make ends meet, and one or both of them may travel for the job, leaving his or her partner to double up on home duties or both of them scrambling to find childcare coverage.

These and other common demands on time often leave little room in daily life for formal adult faith formation. As with those who do not attend church regularly, adult catechetical leaders may find it more effective to reach these busy churchgoers with independent learning opportunities that can conform more easily to their schedules. Independent learning is also better suited to aging parishioners who no longer want to travel in less-than-desirable conditions, and to members of the parish who are homebound. Every Catholic is entitled to ongoing faith formation. For many of them, providing independent learning opportunities is often the best way for a catechetical leader to meet that obligation.

Sister Angela Ann Zukowski, MHSH, who has been a pioneer in the field of online learning, says that parishes need to prepare a menu of opportunities that complement peoples' complex lifestyles today. At the same time, she sees that, given adults' changing calendars from week to week, it is becoming increasingly difficult for parishes to plan onsite learning opportunities. For these reasons, she says, "This is where independent learning blossoms!"[65]

AMERICAN RELIGIOUS INDIVIDUALISM FOSTERS SELF-DIRECTED SPIRITUAL SEEKERS

A strong strain of religious individualism courses through much of American history, right up to the present time. Thomas Jefferson said, "I am a sect myself"; Thomas Paine is quoted as saying, "My mind is my church"; and Henry David Thoreau, Walt Whitman, and Ralph Waldo Emerson were all nineteenth-century advocates of American religious individualism.

It is not uncommon today to hear someone say, "I'm spiritual but not religious," meaning that he or she is forging his or her own way when it comes to the spiritual life and religious beliefs. Not too long ago, I heard a popular recording star respond to an interview question about his religious leanings with, "I am not into designer religions." He went on to emphasize that he is walking his own spiritual path.

Sociologist Robert Bellah calls this "doing-my-own-thing" attitude about religion "Sheilaism," a term used by one of his research subjects, Sheila Larson. She told the interviewer, "I believe in God. I'm not a religious fanatic. I can't remember the last time I went to church. My faith has carried me a long way. It's Sheilaism. Just my own little voice."[66]

While Catholicism in America was for a long time relatively immune to the kind of religious individualism that has affected much of Protestantism, the loss of a Catholic subculture has made Catholics, especially younger ones, more vulnerable to assuming an independent attitude about religion. Today, it is not uncommon to hear younger Catholics speak of themselves as spiritual seekers. Because spiritual seekers do not see themselves as confined by religious boundaries, they are generally more open to exploring ways of bringing deeper spiritual meaning into their lives. And because they revel in self-discovery, they are prime candidates for independent or self-directed learning.

THE INTERNET IS CHANGING THE EDUCATIONAL PARADIGM

With the advent of the personal computer in the early 1980s, the educational paradigm began a seismic shift. The changes were slow in coming at first, but they quickly picked up speed, especially as web technology advanced. According to the Sloan Consortium, an online education advocacy group, nearly four million students took at least one online course in 2007, a 12 percent increase from the previous year. Today, there is hardly a college or university that does not offer online courses or, for that matter, an entire degree program via the Internet.

This point was driven home to me on a flight from Los Angeles to Baltimore. During a service break in the long flight, I spotted a flight attendant doing what appeared to be homework. When I remarked on her activity, she informed me that she was pursuing an online degree. She said that given her constant travel from city to city, she could not pursue a more traditional curriculum.

The Internet has made it possible for people to pursue continuing education from any place and at any time. Learning is no longer bound by who stands before the learners and by what he or she knows. Indeed, the Massachusetts Institute of Technology has placed its entire curriculum online. A viewer can access even the most sophisticated courses without paying a fee, unless he or she wants credit hours. And Google has reached an agreement that enables it to continue its efforts to make every book in the English language text-searchable. The point is that information is expanding exponentially and is increasingly accessible for anyone who uses a computer.

It is, however, not just that more information is at our fingertips; it is how that information can be worked with that is also influencing the learning process. With Web 2 technology, learning is no longer a one-way process: information given, information received. Learners are growing accustomed to making content as well as learning it. The online encyclopedia

Wikipedia and open-source software, such as Linux, are prime examples of how learners are simultaneously drawing from content as well as adding to it. Educators who continue to see learning as a one-way enterprise will be left in the dust.

Colleges and universities are scrambling to catch up in course offerings, formats, and techniques for today's multitasking digital learners. According to educational innovator Marc Prensky, young people who were born after the dawn of the computer age are what he terms "digital natives."[67] Their neural passages are literally being shaped as they mature in ways that enable them to handle more expeditiously digital material of increasing complexity. By contrast, says Prensky, the rest of us (including most college professors) are "digital immigrants." We may learn how to use efficiently many of today's digital resources, but we'll never be native speakers of the digital language, like those who grew up with the computer.

Adult catechetical leaders are not immune to these developments. While religious instruction has its established methods, which have proven highly effective for its purpose, the changing mindset of the "new" learner must be taken seriously. "Would you like to attend a lecture by Father Smith this Wednesday on Catholic social justice principles?" "Ah . . . don't think so. I'm kinda interested in the topic, but I'll just Google it when I get the chance." This type of exchange is likely to become more and more common, especially as today's young adults take center-stage in the Catholic population. There is a growing awareness that if a program is only about information, it is probably not worth the trouble attending, because that information can most likely be gotten more quickly and easily in other ways, especially online.

Onsite programs have to offer other benefits besides information in order to attract attendees. The benefits, such as face-to-face communication, learning from others, experiencing community, shared prayer, and hospitality are often there, but they must be intentional in the program's design and explicit in its promotion. Otherwise, it is a simple choice between either getting information quickly at one's convenience or sitting through a lecture for the better part of an evening. And that's an easy choice to make for an increasing number of Catholics.

The fact is that using a search engine such as Google or Ask.com is the way most computer users get their information today. It is quick, self-directed, and wonderfully open-ended. Following links can lead the learner to related areas that were unforeseen before the search began, but now yield additional information quite beneficial to the learning process.

When my sister-in-law landed in the hospital with a diagnosis of acute leukemia, her older son who was away at college sped to her bedside within hours. She could not understand why he was so distraught since the doctors had not yet briefed her on her prognosis or their plan of attack on the disease. But he had already researched her condition online and knew her situation was grim. She died within two years.

Before the Internet, only medical personnel would have known what my sister-in-law was facing, and the family would have learned of her condition only when the doctors were ready to disclose it. Her son retrieved that information within minutes and without the benefit of medical personnel. That is an example of how dramatically the learning paradigm is shifting in today's fast-changing world. Information is no longer reserved for the experts, including Church officials and theologians.

Certainly, there are potential and real problems with people misunderstanding what they are reading, especially when it comes to esoteric information. Fortunately, in my nephew's case, he had the wisdom to understand the limits of his medical knowledge and never said a word about what he had discovered to his mother. That will not be as true with other learners who will jump ahead to faulty conclusion, whether it is about medicine or Church teaching.

Still, the fact remains that virtually unlimited information is available to learners, and adult catechetical leaders will need to decide how best to make use of this new learning paradigm.

They can try to control information by offering only onsite programming; or, they can tap the energy and potential of the new paradigm, despite its risks, by promoting more independent learning. An additional reason for their doing so is the fact that undereducated learners are four times more likely than those with more education to withdraw from educational programs. But they are as likely to engage in self-directed programs as those with higher education.

MISSION WARRANTS A RETHINKING OF APPROACHES TO ADULT FAITH FORMATION

Jesus said, "Go and teach." We say, essentially, "Come and learn." As the Church grew in numbers and became more institutionalized, it was only natural that the teaching paradigm shifted from missionary outreach to localized instruction. The most efficient way to reach a large number was to gather them in one place.

But as noted above, this paradigm is being subjected to considerable stress from a variety of factors. Moving in the direction of supporting independent learning is becoming a much more attractive option than it was a few years ago. Before the Internet, the best that could be done to support independent learning was to have a good parish library and a well-stocked vestibule reading rack. Today, information from top-tier university databases to the Vatican's published resources are but a few clicks away.

From the Second Vatican Council on, there has been considerable emphasis placed—rightly so—on the central, if not irreplaceable, role that the parish community plays in the catechetical process. As a result, many catechetical leaders have been reluctant to envision substantial adult faith formation taking place outside the immediate confines of the parish community. But helping self-directed learners should not be seen as separating their faith formation from the community, but rather as extending the community's teaching mission to all of its members, some of whom cannot avail themselves of its onsite services. The challenge, as we shall see, is how to ensure that self-directed learning is linked back to the community as much as possible.

SELF-DISCOVERY IS AT THE HEART OF SPIRITUAL LEARNING

As Catholics, we are the beneficiaries of the Church's Magisterium, its authoritative teaching voice. Down through its history, the Church has had to grapple with countless issues of life and faith, the results of which have led to the development of a rich treasury of theological content and doctrine.

The downside of having such a rich source of authoritative teaching is that we can unwittingly use it in ways that co-opt the learner's need for inner work, which is essential for his or her personal transformation. Some teaching methods, such as Shared Praxis, developed by Dr. Thomas Groome of Boston College, seek to achieve a creative balance between self-directed inquiry and the instructive voice of the Church. Unfortunately, many adult faith formation programs become weighted down with too much input about what the Church teaches at the expense of too little opportunity for reflection and analysis. It is the proper balance that makes all the difference in the ongoing process of conversion.

We have no better example of this than Jesus' approach to teaching. He used a variety of teaching methods, such as parables, stories, symbols, metaphors, and gestures, all of which were intended to stimulate, if not jar, people's thinking. He was more interested in uprooting their assumptions and stirring their feelings than he was having them grasp only intellectually what he was saying. He wanted conversion in their hearts as well as understanding in their heads.

One of Jesus' favorite tactics was to provoke thinking through the use of questions. The author of the Gospel of John presents Jesus as an almost Socratic figure, who asks lots of questions to get people to think. Sometimes, such as with the questions about who one's neighbor is and what is owed Caesar, Jesus confounds his listeners by answering the question with a question. He wants his listeners to grapple with the issues and not simply rely on the information he gives them. He wants them, in effect, to be self-directed learners. Jesus knew that thinking is driven by questions, not by answers.

Sometimes as adult catechetical leaders, we are too knowledgeable for our own good about what we teach. We fall to the temptation of filling the learning space with our words, our grasp of the issues. We too readily provide answers from our storehouse of information instead of posing questions or using other methods, such as journaling and group discussion, to stimulate thinking and facilitate self-directed inquiry.

As was noted earlier, the desert fathers had a saying: "Go to your cell. It will teach you everything." They knew that to grow spiritually you have to grapple with your inner demons, those thoughts and prejudices that hold back illumination and conversion. Similarly, Sufi teachers would first send learners away to struggle with spiritual or religious issues on their own prior to engaging them in instruction. They also had the saying, "Words have to die if humans are to live"—a reminder that self-directed inquiry is the bedrock of spiritual learning.

A number of years ago, when I was responsible for adolescent catechesis in our parish, part of one year's curriculum focused on world religions. A special feature of the curriculum was trips to various religious sites where the youth would meet and learn from leaders of other faith traditions. In preparing for our visit to a Buddhist temple, I traveled there beforehand to talk with the monks about what we hoped to accomplish when the students came. The monk who greeted me at the door ushered me into the main temple area where he said the students would be brought. After some polite exchanges, I brought up the students who would be coming and recommended that he give them an overview on Buddhism prior to opening the floor for questions and discussion.

The monk looked at me with soft eyes that began to narrow as his face broadened into a gentle smile of amusement. He then said, "That is not the Buddhist way. We do not speak about things that the learners may not be interested in or have questions about. When your students come, we will bring them here, into this room. They will look around and see the Buddha and all the other things that symbolize our beliefs, including these robes I wear. Then their minds will start filling with questions. And when they are ready to learn, they will start asking their questions. It is then that I will speak. Their questions are the way for how Buddhism will become more known to them." I learned an important lesson that day about the proper balance between giving information and supporting self-directed inquiry.

For authentic spiritual learning, there needs to arise within the learner an inner authority that comes from him or her "inhabiting" the subject. It cannot come solely from information infused from the outside. It has to be owned and integrated into one's person in order for conversion to occur. Self-directed learning is a vital component of contemporary adult faith formation, whether as part of an onsite program or as an independent learning experience. All good adult catechesis is self-directed at its most fundamental level.

How to Develop and Support Independent or Self-directed Learning

GET HELP

Making a concerted effort to provide independent learning opportunities will require time and energy. It is not something that can easily be thrown together or done as an afterthought. Adult catechetical leaders and their committees will need to allocate human and financial resources to the task, just as they do for onsite programming.

When websites became readily available to the mass market, virtually every organizational leader could see their potential for extending an organization's mission into people's offices and homes. What many of them didn't realize, however, is just how much time, energy, cost, and expertise website development and maintenance would require. A similar miscalculation should not be made about digitally based independent learning. If you are going to offer digital learning opportunities, you will need to do your homework about what it will take to create and sustain such an endeavor.

A good way to begin is to get "digital natives" involved. These are young people who have a firsthand grasp of the Internet's potential for serving independent learning. Besides, this is a wonderful strategy for pulling them into parish ministry in a way that is right up their alley. Tell them what you want to accomplish, and let them come back to you with several proposals. Consider the proposals carefully, weighing the pros and cons of each. Then, when you have your plan clearly in mind, especially about possible roles these young "experts" can play, turn them loose. Your task, in part, will be to steer their creative efforts toward results that you would otherwise not be able to achieve on your own.

At the same time, parish catechetical leaders fortunately do not have to do everything from scratch. There are many high-quality online programs that will meet a variety of parishioners' learning interests. For example, the University of Dayton's Institute for Pastoral Initiatives has created the Virtual Learning Community for Faith where people can access faith formation courses. The University of Notre Dame's S.T.E.P. program offers online theology courses and lectures, as do Boston College's C-21 online courses for spiritual enrichment and faith renewal. Catholic Distance University in Hampton, Virginia, was founded exclusively as an online program and offers a variety of degree and non-degree programs. These are but a few of the burgeoning online opportunities available to the Catholic community.

CREATE COMMUNICATION CHANNELS

Since you are trying, at least in part, to reach adults who may not regularly attend church, think about how you are going to get information to them on self-directed learning opportunities. If they don't come to you, you have to go to them. Here are some suggestions:

- Send home information with children who are dropped off for church services or religious education. Many parents don't attend church but insist that their children have some religious formation.

- Have wives and husbands take home information to their mates who are not attending church but who might be open to exploring an interesting topic through independent learning.

- Ask parishioners to take home flyers to Catholic neighbors and friends who live in the parish but do not regularly attend.

- If the parish has an e-mail list for parishioners, use it to announce learning opportunities.

- Make the parish website so compelling that it is a must see. (Transfiguration Parish in Marietta, Georgia, now does its own newscasts on the Web. Parishioners tune in frequently to see what is going on in the highly active parish. Adult faith formation opportunities are often featured.[68])

- Use the parish census-taking or parish visitation programs to drop off information about adult faith formation.

- Buy inexpensive space in community news-papers to highlight topics that are available through independent learning.

- Encourage parishioners to spread the word about resources they have utilized in their study that they have found beneficial. Perhaps you can create an online space for this type of exchange.

- Find out how various populations within the parish access and share information, and then tap into those channels. Laundromats, beauty salons, barbershops, corner markets, and recreation centers are good places to place information about upcoming learning opportunities, especially for immigrant communities.

IDENTIFY THE LEARNING OPPORTUNITIES

When it comes to learning, most adults are interested in their life-task issues more than anything else. This includes their general well-being and spirituality. As I describe in the final chapter, a well-designed needs analysis should help bring to the surface important issues that can be addressed through learning. At the same time, pay attention to the news media, which are always good at identifying what is on people's minds. If they broadcast or publish it, you can bet people are thinking about it.

The best approach to presenting a topic is to introduce it with questions. The idea is to connect with the learner's felt needs about the topic at hand. Take for example the topic of prayer. Here is how that topic might be introduced in a parish bulletin or flyer for self-directed learning:

- Do you sometimes struggle with prayer?

- Do you find your mind unable to focus when you pray?

- Do you feel guilty about how little you pray?

- Do you wonder if God even pays attention to you when you pray?

- Do you wonder why your prayers never seem to get answered?

If you can identify with one or more of these questions, then take advantage of our self-directed course on prayer. You can learn how to pray better right in the convenience of your home. The program comes with a DVD and helpful print material on family prayer activities. The course has eight sessions and generally spans about four weeks when the prayer exercises are practiced.

Stop by, call, or e-mail the religious education office to reserve a copy or to get more information about the program. Reviews by parishioners who have already used the program are available on our Website at (*insert Web address*).

In this example, the idea is to use questions to provoke people's reflection about their prayer life and how it is going. From that reflection, they are in a better position to consider what your program can possibly do for them. A simple description of the program without first trying to get them to reflect on their own experience of prayer is far less effective as a promotional strategy.

This strategy can also be used to link any topic with the higher education program offerings described above. But it is incumbent upon adult catechetical leaders to first familiarize themselves with those programs before suggesting them as resources to meet specific needs.

IDENTIFY RESOURCES

Planning independent or self-directed learning experiences is similar to planning onsite programs. Once you have identified the topics you want to cover, it is important to identify the resources that will best serve that need. When it comes to an onsite program, this generally proves to be a fairly manageable task: Do we go with this or that speaker, this or that film, this or that book? But when it comes to the Internet, a veritable world of resources is at your fingertips.

Here again, it would be good to invite parishioner participation. Following general guidelines you provide, they can surf the Web, looking at the most promising sites for continuing faith formation. Many of these will be Catholic-sponsored, and others will not. The point is to find out what is available to best serve as a resource for a specific need, regardless of origin.

Sr. Angela Ann Zukowski, whom I cited earlier, says that the adult faith formation leader needs to see herself or himself as the conductor of a vast symphony of resources to which he or she can direct learners based upon their specific perceived needs and interests. "Thus, the adult faith formation leader or parish catechetical leader is required to be on constant alert for new, available resources within the public Catholic forum to include in their kaleidoscope of parish offerings."

Some of the most valuable resources available are, in fact, not specifically Catholic but nonetheless provide material that harmonizes well with Catholic belief and practices. For example, many Catholics follow *Speaking of Faith* with NPR's Krista Tipett. An excellent interviewer, Tipett explores topics of faith from a wide range of viewpoints. Many of her interviewees are Catholic leaders and theologians. What makes *Speaking of Faith* an attractive resource for independent learning is that its sessions are archived and can be downloaded onto an MP3 player to be listened to while exercising, traveling, or doing housework. The transcripts of the interviews are also available online.[69]

The National Cathedral in Washington, D.C., sponsors *Sunday Forum*, an interview program that can be watched live online each Sunday morning or accessed later through the archives. Samuel T. Lloyd, the dean of the National Cathedral and an excellent interviewer, hosts religious leaders of all backgrounds, including Catholics. The National Cathedral also archives its sermons, which are a valuable resource because they are based upon the same lectionary we use as Catholics.[70]

The Internet, of course, is not the only source of resources, although it is certainly the largest. There are books, magazines, films, and diocesan newspapers, which syndicate, for example, Catholic News Service's *Faith Alive* articles. And many times, the Public Broadcasting Station and other channels will run specials on the life of Christ, such as PBS *Frontline's* "From Jesus to Christ."

Another valuable resource for independent learning is The Teaching Company (www.teach12.com), which offers over fifty high-level courses in its religion category. Topics range from scripture, to Jesus, to the papacy, to world religions. The courses are available on CD/DVD, tape, or through download, and the instructors are noted leaders in their respective disciplines.

An adult catechetical leader should pay close attention to what is happening in the lives of his or her parishioners and have a good handle on available learning resources. It is the linking of these two points of awareness that often brings about the best and most relevant programming for learners.

OTHER PROGRAM CONSIDERATIONS

In offering self-directed learning opportunities, consider providing a brief self-study guide if one does not already come with the recommended resource. A few reflection questions and suggestions for applying the learning can prove very beneficial to learners. Important, too, is information on related material that can be found in the *Catechism of the Catholic Church* or the *United States Catholic Catechism for Adults*.[71] This would help the learner situate the topic being studied within the broader framework of the Catholic story.

Also think of the learner's need for follow-up. Contact information and a place to go with questions helps link the learner to the broader parish community. Invite the learner to evaluate the experience so that revisions can be made to the program. If the learner is willing to have his or her evaluations posted online, then other potential users of the program or resource can also benefit from the experience.

Amazon it; that is, use Amazon's technique of saying, in effect, people who read this book also read x, y, and z. Only in this case, it would be "people who took this course also studied . . . " The point is to keep bringing before the learner new self-directed learning possibilities for expanding their faith understanding.

Be sure to always convey a "we care about you" tone in all your dealings with independent learners. Let them know that the parish is interested in them and would like to help them in whatever ways it can. Use every opportunity to link the independent learner with the parish community and its other activities.

Start modestly. Begin with a group of interested persons who would be willing to experiment with the program and give honest feedback. If the program proves successful, have them give witness to the experience. They will prove to be your best marketing strategy.

ONSITE SELF-DIRECTED PROGRAMS

Not all self-directed learning takes place apart from the parish. Many onsite programs have self-directed dimensions to them. For example, when I was a parish catechetical leader, I had a dozen or so adult learning groups working simultaneously. They each decided on their own topics and secured their own resources.

Groups of this nature can easily be launched in any parish. Sometimes it is helpful if the groups can use a discussion guide and selected resources to get underway. But after a while, it is my experience that once groups get some experience meeting as learners, they will develop their own agendas. My wife and I participate in a discussion group that has been meeting for over twenty-five years. It started as part of the parish's *From Ashes to Easter* program but continued on after the program concluded. The group meets monthly about a topic selected by the host couple, who also provides the reading or viewing material.

Intergenerational or family groups can also be self-directed. Our family met for years as part of the parish's *Learning in Faith Together* program. This was started to enable families to bring other dimensions to the catechetical process. Four or five families met monthly for catechetical instruction. The gatherings were concluded with a shared meal. A number of the learning activities included outreach to homeless shelters and food pantries. Each group worked with the religious education office to prepare its curriculum and secure learning resources, but beyond that, the learning was self-directed.

That more and more learning today is self-directed has significant implications for adult faith formation. Adult catechetical leaders will need to develop learning experiences that respond to this increasingly preferred learning style. And while independent learning presents opportunities to reach parishioners who might otherwise not attend an onsite program, it does have its challenges. It will take time and care to ensure that it is done well, that it is faithful to the Catholic story, and that it stays suitably linked to the faith community that sponsors it.

Reflection Questions

1. What attracts you most about independent learning for adult faith formation?

2. What concerns might you have about moving more in the direction of independent learning in your parish?

3. What preliminary steps would you need to take to make independent learning a greater part of your adult faith formation?

4. What might be some obstacles to your offering more independent learning?

5. How well do you think your parishioners would respond to independent learning opportunities?

6. What are some ways you can build independent learning components into your onsite programs?

7. How did you feel about the section on self-discovery's essential role in spiritual learning? Did it resonate with your personal experience?

CHAPTER 6

Turning Vision into Reality

As I have pointed out in some detail in previous chapters, today's adult catechetical leader needs to pay more attention to serving the independent learning needs and preferences of contemporary adults. This includes helping adults attend more frequently and effectively to the teaching voice of God.

At the same time, there is no substitute for a parish's having a well-designed, well-functioning adult faith formation program. After all, the parish is the central gathering place of the local believing community, and it is within this context that adults can make great strides in deepening their faith knowledge and commitment. In this chapter, we will look at what is involved in constructing a successful adult faith formation program in the parish. Additional assistance is available to you through another book in this series, *A Concise Guide to Pastoral Planning* by Dr. William Pickett. That book addresses steps for pastoral planning that reach beyond the specific tasks pertinent to adult formation ministry, but much of it will easily transfer to this area of Church life. Pickett offers excellent guidance for information gathering, needs assessment, goal and objective setting, and evaluation.

We turn now to eight basic steps to building an adult faith formation program:

1. Establish, train, and support an adult faith formation committee or team.

2. Assess the "teachings" or messages that are already going on in the life and mission of the parish.

3. Help the learners identify what it is that they want or need to learn.

4. Establish overall goals and specific objectives that would serve the learning needs and mission of the parish.

5. Design the program in accordance with the learning outcomes desired.

6. Promote the program.

7. Implement the program.

8. Evaluate the degree to which the learning outcomes were achieved.

The eighth step automatically feeds back into the third step, which is to determine the learning needs and interests of the parish. In this way, the planning process is ongoing and cyclical. If you do the last step right, as we shall see, you have already begun the process of accomplishing the third step, namely, identifying learning needs.

It is important to point out, too, that although the steps are presented here sequentially, in practice, several of them go on simultaneously. Generally, this is not a problem in that most experienced parish catechetical leaders are quite accustomed to having several balls in the air at the same time. It comes with the job. Let's hope, however, that the following steps will at least make that juggling job a little easier.

1. Establish, train, and support an adult faith formation committee or team.

The most important thing a parish catechetical leader can do to get a viable program off the ground is to create, train, and support a well-functioning adult faith formation committee or team. In many dioceses, training programs on adult faith formation are offered to both professionals and volunteers. Where these are available, they should be taken advantage of. But where no such training opportunities exist, it is important for parish leadership to do whatever is necessary to ensure that those who volunteer for adult faith formation ministry receive adequate training. What goes into the development of an adult faith committee will return to the parish in the form of effective ministry to adult learners. This is no place to spare expenses.

PURPOSES

The parish adult faith formation team has four main purposes:

1. to advocate for adult catechesis as a major priority within the parish;

2. to provide opportunities for parish adults to further their growth in faith through a variety of learning experiences;

3. to collaborate with other parish ministries to provide a well-coordinated approach to lifelong learning through such learning formats as intergenerational and whole community catechesis;

4. and to assist other ministries with their training and development needs by helping them with learning designs and resources.

COMPOSITION

The composition of the committee or team should reflect that of the adult population of the parish as much as possible, especially when it comes to young adults and minorities. These populations are often underrepresented on parish committees. At the same time, it is important to recruit individuals who know how to work well on a committee. Despite having desirable talents, some people are not well suited to serve on committees. You want people who are active listeners, able to compromise, and good at reaching decisions. There is nothing worse than a group of people, however dedicated they are, unable to move an agenda forward.

Groups of six to eight work well and are perhaps optimal for most parishes. However, each catechetical leader will need to determine the appropriate number of team members by taking into account parish size and demographic make-up, as well as demands placed on the committee. I had a much larger group of people on my parish adult faith formation committee, but I broke it down into more manageably sized task groups. This model seems to work well, especially in a large parish where lots of demands for learning activities could overwhelm a small group.

RECRUITMENT/SUPPORT

Personal invitation is most often the best way to secure volunteers. Appeals from the pulpit or in the bulletin rarely work well in isolation. It is preferable that someone who knows of a good candidate for service makes a recommendation that is then followed up with a visit or phone call. The public announcements are important, however, in encouraging those who might not otherwise be identified. Otherwise you run the risk of missing newcomers to the parish and to the ministry.

Before asking someone to serve on the committee, be sure to develop a team member job description. This provides the person with crucial information necessary for discerning whether adult faith formation is a good ministry for him or her. The position description should offer a basic description of the ministry, spell out the core duties of committee service, and indicate both the length of service and the time commitment expected.

Avoid seeking an immediate response from the person you are inviting to serve on the committee. Allow him or her sufficient time to pray about the invitation and to consult other family members about what possible impact committee service might have on family life. Treat the invitation as a calling to official ministry within the parish, because that is what it is. Consequently, allowing time for prayer and discernment are essential components of the recruitment process.

If the person agrees to serve, try to arrange a letter of appointment by the pastor or parish administrator. This should welcome the person as a minister and pledge prayer and support for success. Of course, the letters can be prepared by others and made available for the pastor or parish administrator to sign. Still, as the parish's chief catechist, it is important that he or she know or, if desired, have a say in who is being invited to official parish ministry. (A sample letter of appointment appears in the Appendix.)

Once the committee is staffed, it is imperative that it be adequately trained in the basic theory and practice of adult faith formation. Fortunately, many resources are available for this purpose, including an excellent video published by the National Conference for Catechetical Leadership and produced by RCL/Benziger of Allen, Texas, *Echoes of Faith Plus: Adult Faith Formation–Methodology*.[72]

The literature on volunteer management stresses the need to provide ongoing support for volunteers and to regularly thank them for their contribution. One of the reasons people avoid volunteering is that they feel they might step into a situation where they will be left on their own and unable to easily get out of doing what the pastor and others now expect

of them. People volunteer because they want to make a difference. Periodically checking with them to find out how they feel
about their ministry and what additional support they need
will go a long way to helping them have a good experience. So
will compliments and kind expressions of gratitude.

2. Assess the "teachings" or messages that are already going on in the life and mission of the parish.

Whether or not a single adult education program is offered in
a parish, considerable adult faith formation is taking place. A
parish teaches by the way it mediates Catholic life through its
rituals, structures, services, and community-building activities.
There is virtually no aspect of parish life that does not convey
some value or message about Catholic life: from the way the
receptionist greets callers, to budget allocations, to the extent of
lay leadership, to the way new parishioners are welcomed and
incorporated into the life of the community.

Those who are responsible for adult faith formation in the
parish should consider developing a list of questions that they
can use to assess the kinds of formation that are operative in the
parish. For example, the adult education committee might look
at liturgy through the following questions:

- Do our liturgical celebrations help people live
  the Gospel?

- Do visitors to our parish feel welcome?

- Are there opportunities for celebrating community following Sunday Mass (coffee and donuts,
  fellowship gatherings, friendly conversations in
  the vestibule and/or in the parking lot)?

A Concise Guide to Adult Faith Formation

A question on parish mission might explore such questions as these:

- Do most parishioners know what our parish mission is?

- Does our mission draw us outside ourselves in service to the wider community?

- To what degree are we living our mission?

- Does our budget reflect the values articulated in our mission?

When conducting workshops on adult faith formation, I often hand out a sheet on which some fifteen areas of parish life are identified. I then ask participants from the same parish to discuss what lessons their parishioners are learning in each area through their lived experience of the parish. The participants find it both illuminating and energizing to talk through these things. Not everyone agrees as to what the parish is communicating through, say, liturgy, family life ministry, or social outreach. But they find the exercise helpful in elevating their awareness of the formative influences that are taking place in the life of the community. It is important for adult catechetical leaders to know what is working in their favor and can be built upon in offering learning experiences. Or, if the opposite were true, what forces they are up against. (A sample list of categories for the adult faith formation team to consider about what messages are being transmitted appears in the Appendix.)

As I noted in chapter 2 (on the parish as context for adult formation), if the lived reality of the parish differs substantially from what is said in informational programs, the lived message will trump the spoken word. At the very least, the difference between the two messages will cause in learners what educators call "cognitive dissonance." This is something that hampers learning because the learner is faced with trying to reconcile two conflicting messages. Taking the time to think through the lived messages of a parish will greatly help an adult education committee offer learning experiences that bear good potential for success. If the committee discerns that certain aspects of parish life are giving the wrong message, they can and should bring their findings to the pastor's or parish administrator's attention.

3. Help the learners identify what it is that they want or need to learn.

As noted in the chapter on the adult leaner, adults are independent and free to decide if and what they want to learn. This is why adult educators of all kinds take care to identify the learning needs and desires of the potential learners. Programs that address issues that people are concerned about every day have a far better chance of attracting participants.

Experienced adult religious educators use a variety of methods to discover the learning interests of parishioners. But prior to discussing some of the more popular methods, I would like to return to a point I made earlier. When evaluating how a program went, take the opportunity to ask participants what more they would like to learn about that or similar topics. People who have just benefited from a good learning experience are often more disposed to identifying what it is that they would like to learn next and the manner in which they would like to learn it. Building needs assessment right into the evaluation process means that you will not have to go back to those learners at some later date for information on what and how they want to learn; you can receive excellent feedback while you still have their positive attention.

Assessing learning needs and interests falls into the two broad categories of *less formal* and *more formal*. You will likely find, however, that a mixture of methods will provide the best information.

LESS FORMAL METHODS OF ASSESSING NEEDS AND INTERESTS

This category includes techniques that put emphasis on listening and observing, such as paying attention to what parishioners talk about as they assemble for meetings, social events, and coffee klatches after Mass. Posters and bulletin and pulpit announcements indicating that adult faith formation planning is getting under way can be combined with a suggestion box for parishioners to deposit ideas. Interviews with the pastor or parish administrator, other professional staff members, and volunteer ministers can surface valuable information on issues about which people are concerned. A parish that has a formal program of pastoral visitation has an additional forum in which to easily inquire about learning interests.

I encourage adult catechetical leaders to pay close attention to the media for two key reasons. One is that members of the news media in particular pay attention to what is on people's minds and then address the issues in special reports, magazine articles, TV features, and the like. A second and consequential reason is that once an issue is in the news, people think and talk about it more. For example, if *Time* magazine ran an article entitled "Are teenage girls growing up too fast?" you can bet that this issue is on a lot of your parents' minds. How to address the issue from a faith formation perspective is a key task for catechetical leaders. The point is that the news and other media as well can be valuable fonts of information that catechetical leaders should be vigilant in observing and critiquing. From them, we can learn a great deal about the cultural and social context within which we seek to hand on the faith.

When I was serving as a parish catechetical leader, the Vietnam War was still going on. There was a lot of discussion within our socially active parish about the morality of the war. Feelings sometimes ran hot. I did not need to take a survey as to whether there was any interest in exploring the Church's teachings on peace and just war. Everything I heard in the parish and saw in the media told me that this was an issue that needed to be addressed. I was able to put together a series of programs that analyzed various aspects of the Church's teaching. The attendance was good, and for those who came, a learning need was met.

Finally, in the less formal category, I include the Church's liturgical year and special issues that are highlighted periodically by the Vatican and American bishops. For example, I found that Advent was an opportune time to offer programs on topics such as the birth of the Messiah and the infancy narratives in the New Testament. Lent is a liturgical season pregnant with possibilities because during this time, many parishioners often look for opportunities to do something more spiritual. Programs on various aspects of spirituality, such as learning how to use Centering Prayer, often address felt needs. In these instances, be sure that the programs themselves are enriching spiritual experiences and not just conveyers of information about spiritual matters.

MORE FORMAL METHODS OF ASSESSING NEEDS AND INTERESTS

More formal methods for securing information on parishioner needs and interests include questionnaires, focus groups, telephone interviews, and the post-learning program evaluation opportunities of which I spoke earlier. Of these, the questionnaire is the method most frequently used—and misused.

If I've heard the complaint once, I've heard it scores of times: "I did a questionnaire and got people's input about what they wanted. But when I put the program on, virtually no one showed up." As we shall see as we proceed through the steps of program planning, there are multiple variables that affect people's decision to attend a program. For starters, the program may indeed be a topic someone is interested in, but the program is offered at an inconvenient time, or no childcare is available. An indication of interest on a questionnaire very often does not convert to participation in a program—even one designed specifically to match that interest.

To make matters more complex, creating a questionnaire that secures valid and useful information for program design is not something that you just sit down and knock off in an hour or so. And yet from what I have seen, many parish catechetical leaders are prone to doing just that. Designing a valid questionnaire is something that takes care, some expertise, and ongoing refinement. When it is well done, it can produce very useful information. The Gallup Organization can predict the outcome of a presidential race within a few percentage points by surveying approximately fifteen hundred people across the country. It doesn't take a lot of people to get good information if your survey sample is representative and your questions are valid.

With this in mind, let's look at some general guidelines for building a good questionnaire.

1. Try to secure professional help on designing a valid survey instrument. You may have parishioners who have this expertise as part of their job, or you can access resources at a local library, a nearby college or university, or online.

2. Have committee members identify the kinds of information you want to secure. Do you need demographic information, such as age, gender, education level, computer availability, and childcare needs? Do you want to identify concerns at an emotional level, an intellectual level, or both? Do you want a questionnaire that is easy to tabulate, or could you go more in-depth with some open-ended questions? Hint: A good rule of thumb is to try to make the questionnaire as easy to tabulate as possible with, if needed, a few open-ended questions. Open-ended questions require multiple readers to ensure accurate interpretation of what was said.

3. Develop and continually refine the questions that you think will best elicit the information you desire. Make sure there is only one way for the reader to interpret a question. Any question that is open to multiple interpretations gives

invalid information, since you won't know what understanding of the question the readers had in mind.

4. Keep it simple. If the questionnaire is off-putting to start with, people are not going to be interested in completing it. I have received many questionnaires (by mail or by e-mail) that I chose not to complete simply because they would require too much of my time or they looked more complex than I cared to oblige.

5. When you are basically satisfied with your questionnaire, do a test run with people you can interview afterward. You will be interested in learning from them at least the following information:

   • How long it took them to complete the questionnaire.

   • Their overall feelings about the questionnaire: Were there too many questions? Too complicated?

   • What they understood each question to mean.

   • Did the questionnaire help them identify their concerns, interests, and needs relative to their faith? If not, what is needed to help surface that information?

6. Revise the instrument in accordance with the feedback you got from the test run. Then do another test run to see how well you addressed the issues that were raised.

7. Think of using a random sample of the parish population instead of trying to blanket everyone with a questionnaire. The returns will be much easier to tabulate, and your data will be a more accurate reflection of the parish if you can secure a return of most of the questionnaires. Plan in advance how you will follow up to remind recipients that you are counting on their response.

8. If your parish has a population where computers are available and used in virtually every household, consider an electronic survey. People are much more likely to fill

out a questionnaire that pops up on their screen and looks fairly easy to fill out. But don't use an online survey if you have population pockets that do not have ready access to a computer. Your data will be skewed in favor of those with computers.

4. Establish overall goals and specific objectives that would serve the learning needs and mission of the parish.

In my early years of serving as a parish catechetical leader, I staffed a committee responsible for planning and facilitating an annual retreat for the parish's teenagers. At one of the first planning meetings, I proposed that we identify the overall goals and specific objectives that we wanted to accomplish at the retreat. One of the committee members vigorously opposed the idea, referring to it as a pedantic exercise. He claimed that the committee had in mind the general themes that the retreat would address, and they were sufficient to guide the presenters. But I held my ground, and eventually the committee worked through the specific outcomes that it wanted the retreat to accomplish.

After the retreat, which turned out quite successful, the committee member who originally opposed the idea of identifying objectives told me that he had been wrong. He said that he came to see how important the objectives were in guiding the design and implementation of the retreat and in helping the committee to evaluate its success.

Sometimes, working through the often challenging task of specifying goals and objectives seems like an unnecessary burden in the development of an adult education program. On occasion, we might be tempted to say something like, "Look, I know the topics I want to address, and I've got some great speakers lined up. What's the point of writing up goals and objectives? I've already got the general framework in my head. I know where we are going and how to get there. What else is needed?"

What else is needed is a well-thought-through vision of how the adults in the parish will be served through the accomplishment of specific learning outcomes. These outcomes are not of a general, broad-brush variety; they are clearly identified in terms of knowledge, feelings, and skills. They spell out what you want the participants to walk away with when they finish the program.

Setting goals and objectives is the work of the adult faith formation committee and provides its members with a common blueprint for proceeding with the faith formation program. In this way, everyone can get on board and work both individually and cooperatively to accomplish the program's goals. Guesswork is kept to a minimum, personality conflicts are often avoided, and the personal passions and agendas of individual members can be held accountable or subordinate to the strategic plan itself.

Well-identified learning outcomes have another advantage. They become essential components of promoting the program. If you don't know in specific detail what you want to accomplish with the learners, you cannot adequately describe to potential participants what they can expect to get out of the program. When adults can't readily see the benefits of a particular program, there is little likelihood that they will participate.

WHAT IS THE DIFFERENCE BETWEEN GOALS AND OBJECTIVES?

Goals are general statements of purpose, something that you want to accomplish on a broad scale over an extended period of time. They often span a three- to five-year period. Adult faith formation goals will need to reflect or harmonize with the parish mission or some other major direction that is a current priority. For example, a parish deciding to focus on the family may make helping the family better understand and actualize itself as a "domestic church" a goal for the year. There could, of course, be other goals related to the family in the same calendar year. How many goals a parish identifies for any given period depends on what it thinks it can accomplish with the resources that it has.

Objectives are specific outcomes the parish wants to accomplish as essential stepping-stones in the attainment of its overall goal. Typically, they are to be achieved in the span of about a year. The parish is saying that by accomplishing its objectives (outcomes), it will have accomplished its goal. For example, with regard to the goal on the family as a domestic church, a parish may identify three objectives:

- Designing an adult program on the meaning and benefits of being a domestic church (knowledge-focused).

- Developing a family-based program wherein a family can learn together ways to enhance its life as domestic church (skills-focused).

- Offering a retreat for families to celebrate together their essential place and purpose within the Church universal (feelings-focused).

Objectives need to be detailed enough so that the committee can easily determine if they have been accomplished. For this reason, they should identify a clear, specific outcome to be reached within a determined period of time. Objectives pin down what you want the learners to accomplish by when.

Think of it this way: No collegiate or professional football team would enter a game without a well-defined game plan. They devote enormous amounts of time preparing for what they want to accomplish. Can we treat the ministry of helping adults learn the faith with any less commitment to preparation and the pursuit of excellence? Working through the sometimes arduous task of establishing clear goals and objectives is our commitment to excellence on behalf of echoing the Good News of Jesus Christ.

5. Design the program in accordance with the learning outcomes desired.

It all comes down to this: Will our program design produce the results we identified in our objectives? All of our work on goals and objectives goes up in smoke if we fail to create a program that enables them to be realized. There is a story told about a lost driver asking a Maine farmer how to get back to a certain town. The farmer begins by telling the driver to proceed one way. He then changes his mind and tells him to go a different way. Finally, he stops, rubs his chin and says, "You know what? You can't get there from here."

In adult faith formation, "you can't get there from here" is, regrettably, too often the case. Many times catechetical leaders want to achieve certain learning objectives, but their chosen learning methodologies are poor vehicles for their doing so.

An instructive example is parent programs for children's first sacraments. These programs are offered with the general understanding of helping parents become first catechists of their children in preparing them to receive the sacraments. But when you look at program designs, they too often consist of lectures about the sacraments and liturgical celebration. There is too often little in the design to help parents gain skills in catechizing their children, such as learning through storytelling and connecting everyday activities to sacramental rites, symbols, and meanings. Simply inviting parents to talk as couples or in small groups about what the sacraments mean in their own faith life does much to boost both their skills as catechist as well as their confidence. It also provides an excellent window through which leadership can assess what doctrinal basics these parents might yet need to learn.

Some years ago, training directors in the business community were asked to rank the effectiveness of various methods for meeting different training objectives. They were given the following six training objectives: knowledge acquisition, knowledge retention, participant acceptance, changing attitudes, problem solving skills, and interpersonal skills. In every instance, they ranked the method "lecture with questions" at or near the bottom of effectiveness.

What is the reason? With a lecture, the learner has to rely almost exclusively on hearing to take in the information. Not only that, but important points being made by the speaker are often missed as the learner is occupied trying to absorb an earlier message. There is no pause button in lectures. The speaker moves on, and the learner has to do his or her best to keep pace.

Once the lecture is over, research shows that the retention rate of what we remember drops off dramatically as time passes. This is why adult educators, when using lecture as the preferred method, will back it up with a variety of techniques to enhance knowledge acquisition and retention. These include visual support, such as a chalkboard or PowerPoint®, handouts, question and answer opportunities, group discussion, and a delivery pace that facilitates good note-taking. The more senses that can be engaged in the learning process, the greater the learning. The bottom line in all of this is that the catechetical leader must be aware that some learning methods will serve their desired outcomes well, and others will not. They need to weigh carefully which methods will best accomplish which objectives.

If catechetical leaders want to change learners' hearts, they should not aim their message exclusively at their heads. They have to do things that engage the whole person, especially at a deeper, emotional level. Think of television commercials; they don't try to provide a lot of information as much as they seek to capitalize on our human longings. Wise catechetical leaders understand that they must work with these same longings as divinely intended pathways to God. If, on the other hand, catechetical leaders want the learners to gain skills in, say, Christian parenting, they have to incorporate some kind of hands-on opportunities for them to practice what they want them to do. Who of us would want a surgeon operating on us who only attended lectures?

The Christian faith is not something that can be grasped at its core with head knowledge alone. To truly understand forgiveness, we have to forgive and experience forgiveness. To understand justice, we have to be just and receive justice. It is in the actual living of our faith that we come to know God. As the prophet Jeremiah said, "To know God is to do justice" (Jer 22:16).

"Truth without charity is not God" is how Pascal described the potential gap between knowing about God and knowing God. This is why adult faith formation programs need to employ methodologies that engage the whole learner, not just the intellect. Effective adult faith formation employs methodologies that extend beyond the classroom into ritual and service. Working collaboratively with other parish ministries to nurture the faith life of the whole person is at the heart of contemporary adult faith formation.

In designing the program, keep in mind some of the pertinent issues raised in earlier chapters. For example, adults often benefit from having a little extra time to reconcile new information with past experience or current views. So provide suitable space in the design process for them to do this. This can take multiple forms, such as a specified time for quiet review of notes, a question and answer period, group discussion or journaling.

Another issue, especially for topics that are more religious or spiritual in nature, is to create opportunities for the participants to attend to God's teaching voice. Here again, allowing some space in the design process for reflection, journaling, and the like can underscore God's important role in the learning process.

For years, I was invited each summer to teach an adult faith formation module as part of a master's program at Regis University in Denver. Because I worked with the learners for a day or more, I could give them opportunities to further explore the topics in ways that were special to them. For twenty minutes or so they could go off to journal, quietly share thoughts with a colleague, write a poem, draw something, or even do an interpretative dance. (Remember how Zorba learned best though dance?) When the class reassembled, I invited volunteers to share their insights. I was always amazed as to how creatively the students deepened their own and our understanding of the topic. Poems and journal entries were read, pictures shown, conversations shared, and, yes, dances performed. The important point is that the learners benefited from their having had the opportunity to deepen and integrate their learning. And for some, just having quiet time to discern God's teaching voice was especially beneficial.

ORGANIC DEVELOPMENT OF CATECHESIS

"Catechesis must have an organic development and cannot be merely episodic."[73]

If there is a major challenge for contemporary adult faith formation, it is this: Short of adults taking a degree in theology or some similar set of studies, how do adult catechetical leaders provide them with a holistic and integrated understanding of their Catholic faith? In responding to their expressed needs and addressing the important issues that invariably arise, how do catechetical leaders go beyond a faith formation process that is basically episodic, with one topic covered here, another one addressed over there? How do adults gain an overall picture of the faith that has the necessary various doctrinal components connected harmoniously to one another?

When bishops, pastors, and other Church leaders complain that Catholics don't know their faith, I believe that their concern stems primarily from the fact that many Catholics have little or no grasp of their faith's meta-narrative, its overarching story that ties everything together. Without knowing how various aspects of their faith relate to one another, they find it difficult to adequately grasp and talk about. They may know this or that aspect of their faith, but they don't have an integrated, holistic understanding of it to serve as an energizing and guiding force in their lives.

There is no easy answer to this problem, but let me suggest several possibilities. First, we now have the *United States Catholic Catechism for Adults*, which is based upon the universal *Catechism of the Catholic Church* and its condensed *Compendium of the Catechism of the Catholic Church*. These resources provide the comprehensive and well-integrated overview of the faith that is so essential to mature belief. Whenever and wherever possible, adult catechetical leaders should direct adult learners to these books. They can serve as the basis of programs about the faith or as important resources for when other issues are addressed. The point is to keep bringing adult parishioners' attention to the catechisms as important resources through which to deepen their faith understanding.

Second, as programs are offered throughout the year, it would be helpful to contextualize each topic in the Church's broader meta-narrative. Written program descriptions can do some of this, as can what is said by way of remarks at the start or conclusion of the program. Also, speakers can be asked to situate their topics within the Church's meta-narrative as a means of better grounding the learning. Discussions about potential follow-up topics, moreover, can allude to related topics as they appear in the catechisms.

The important point is that adult catechetical leaders should not present topics as if they are freestanding entities. Each topic illuminates and is illuminated by other aspects of the faith to which it is related. Good program design ensures that adult learners are regularly enlightened about the systematic and holistic nature of the Catholic faith. Adult faith formation is perhaps best envisioned as a vast and intricate web of discovery, learning, and integration that continues to transform the adult disciple's heart, mind, and behavior throughout their whole of life.

6. Promote the Program

A classic question that shows up time and again at training sessions on adult faith formation is, "How do I motivate adults to attend our programs?" This question is revealing from two standpoints. The first is that it seems to imply that there is some formula or technique for getting parishioners to the programs; and if that formula were known, attendance could be improved. The question also assumes that motivation is triggered from the outside—as in "If you build it, they will come." Buddhists see the matter differently: "When the learner is ready, the teacher will appear" is a common Buddhist expression about learner readiness. In other words, motivation is more about what takes place internally rather than externally. Whatever stimulates and directs motivation, understanding and harnessing it are not easy tasks. Still, we do know we are not without guidance as to what influences it.

Indiana University professors Leon McKenzie and Travis Shipp researched why Catholic adults did *not* attend adult faith formation programs. They discovered that some 16 percent of those they surveyed had a negative mindset about education. In other words, they either saw themselves as too old to learn or were turned off to learning by their past experiences. Around 13 percent of those surveyed reported that they stayed away because they were alienated from Church teaching or practice. Another 19 percent indicated that they were basically non-joiners. Around 10 percent said that they felt estranged from the mainstream of the parish; they didn't see themselves as part of the "in" group that influences much of what happens in the parish. Roughly 18 percent reported that the programs did not meet their needs or interests or were scheduled at inconvenient times. Another 20 percent cited busy schedules and other family or social responsibilities. Finally, a small percentage (3.5) identified physical incapacity as a reason for not attending.

The variety of responses makes it clear that catechetical leaders will need to work on several fronts to improve attendance at adult education events. While there is no simple motivational strategy that will apply across the board, certainly one approach is to be sure to offer programs that meet learners' needs and interests. If they are not attracted to what's being offered, they simply won't come. This is why the planning process begins with needs analysis. The challenge of every aspect of pastoral ministry is to link faith with life. As was mentioned in an earlier chapter, ministry is less about drawing people out of their daily lives into sacred space and more about helping them discover the sacred in their lives. Programs that can successfully do this have a built-in motivational dimension.

Closely related to this is another point raised earlier, namely, the importance of being able to present the benefits of attending a program. Look at virtually any professional development seminar brochure and you will immediately see that the benefits of attending the program are clearly identified. The program sponsors know that unless they put the program's benefits right up front and support them with a money-back guarantee, potential participants will not be willing to pay the high fees these seminars usually command.

In this regard, I often think of Jesus' comment that "the children of this world are more astute than the children of light" (Lk 16:8). I take this to mean that those of us who labor in the realm of the spiritual can learn a lot from those who do not. If those who make a living training others understand the motivational necessity of letting people know beforehand what they can expect to gain from attending, why do we often fail to do similarly? I don't think it is simply because we feel that we deal in matters immeasurable, such as one's relationship with God. That is true enough, but there are outcomes we can and should identify, such as new information, expanded understanding, and new skills. The fact that we frequently fail to identify these benefits is, I think, primarily a reflection of our failure to be clear and precise about the outcomes our program is designed to achieve. If we have not identified them for ourselves, we cannot use them as motivational hooks to draw people to our programs. It is that simple.

On another front, adult catechetical leaders need to pay attention to their program's overall purpose and image. A single-dimension program, such as one that provides information on a particular topic, will be less attractive than a program that includes other faith-enriching dimensions. Attractive programming integrates learning with prayer, community building, critical analysis, and other dimensions of healthy and vibrant Church life. These other dimensions should be promoted as part of a program's benefits. This is especially true in a liturgical season like Lent.

The McKenzie/Shipp research also suggests that the character of parish life has a significant influence on motivation. As we discussed in the chapter on the parish, there is a direct correlation between the quality of parish life and parishioners' interest in educational programming. A parish that is basically lifeless, has uninspiring liturgies, little outreach to parishioners—particularly the marginalized—and has no mission to the wider community is going to find it difficult to attract adults to ongoing faith formation. If parishioners are uninspired on Sunday, there is little to motivate them to turn out on Monday.

Another implication of the McKenzie/Shipp research is the need to create a parish ambiance that disposes parishioners to learn. It is difficult, if not impossible, to stir parishioners to attend educational offerings if ongoing learning is not perceived as an important aspect of faith life. By ambiance I mean parish leadership style, financial priorities, learning facilities, events, posters, announcements, and so forth. All these things together proclaim an unmistakable message: Discipleship warrants lifelong learning, and this parish takes that responsibility seriously.

Even with a good parish environment and a well-developed positive orientation to learning, motivation to attend programs can be negatively affected by schedules and other logistical realities of contemporary life. Many parents face enormous demands on their time getting their kids to and from organized activities, such as dancing class, music lessons, sports events, and recitals. Adult catechetical leaders need to be sensitive to such realities and respond with creative planning and scheduling.

A religious sister on our parish staff started an adult faith formation group for first-time mothers. They met at a time in the day when they felt they could more easily bundle up and bring their newborns along. The format proved so successful that when additional children started arriving, they made necessary adjustments in their schedules and childcare arrangements to keep meeting. They were still meeting when some of the children entered high school.

Another sister I read about joined parishioners who rode the train from New Jersey to their jobs in New York City every weekday. They would meet in a particular car where she would lead them in discussing pre-arranged topics. After the parishioners disembarked for their jobs, Sister would ride the train back home. In some parishes, parishioners who work in the same factory or in close proximity gather for a discussion over a brown bag lunch. It just takes a little creative organizing by catechetical leaders to initiate these kinds of small groups or to promote self-directed learning.

The important thing to keep in mind about the McKenzie/Shipp research is that their statistical breakdown of reasons why people don't attend adult faith formation programs is true of most parishes. It is therefore important for adult catechetical leaders and their committees to discuss what they can do in each category to lessen resistance to attendance. Motivational strategies are not only about stimulating interest but are also about lessening the reasons for non-participation.

When it comes to designing and distributing promotional materials, leaders must be creative and use a variety of approaches. The pulpit and bulletin announcements are worthwhile but highly limited in effectiveness. Keep in mind that given all the junk mail that comes into the average parishioner's house, your material will need to stand out. In this regard, images and logos are more powerful than words. And, don't forget, it is about telling them the benefits of participating.

If you have minority populations, try to find out what works best for these groups in terms of their communication preferences and motivation. Many times it is the recommendations of recognized leaders in the community that influence their participation in an event. Also, announcements posted in laundromats, on grocery store bulletin boards, or at favorite gathering places might get more attention than those in the parish bulletin.

When all is said and done, there is probably nothing more motivational than someone you like calling to say that he or she is interested in a particular program and is wondering if you would like to join him or her. I have more than once attended an event in which I was only half-interested because one or more of my friends invited me to tag along. I was never sorry I did so. The program may have left something to be desired, but the company more than made up for it. Adult catechetical leaders who can stimulate that kind of social networking will experience fewer problems with attendance.

7. Implement the Program

When I worked at the United States Conference of Catholic Bishops, I often had to fly on small regional airplanes. Given their small size, they made a lot of my fellow passengers nervous, but I enjoyed the experience. Whenever I could, I would sit in the front row right behind the pilots. In the days prior to the terror attacks of September 11, there was no door separating the crew from the passengers on these small planes, and I would watch intently as the pilots went through their pre-takeoff procedures using a check-off list.

Living in Washington, D.C., I was all too aware of the importance of going through a checklist. On January 13, 1982, an Air Florida plane crashed a few miles from my home upon takeoff. The cause of the accident was attributed to pilot error. Frustrated by snowstorm delays, the pilots failed to go back through the list to ensure that the internal anti-icing devices were turned on. Seventy-eight people lost their lives as a result.

It is utterly surprising to me how many people will put on programs—some of them quite large—without the benefit of a checklist. A custom-made checklist is one of the best things that adult catechetical leaders can develop and use to ensure that their programs come off without a hitch. A good checklist will include specific entries under such headings as personnel (who needs to do what when), audiovisual resources, printed materials, equipment, hospitality, and publicity.

How many times have we all been in a room waiting for a program to begin while people are still fiddling with the sound system or trying to get the PowerPoint® presentation to work? A good checklist with timelines built in would have prevented such delays and saved the program providers embarrassment. (A sample checklist is provided in the Appendix.)

THINK DEFENSIVELY

When I graduated from college and started my professional career with Pacific Telephone and Telegraph in Los Angeles, I was required to take a defensive driving course. It was called that because the course was designed around the conviction that we drive most safely when we drive with our guard up—in other words, driving in a way that enables us to anticipate, and so avoid, problems.

When it comes to implementing programs, think defensively. Think what would happen if the speaker didn't show up. Think what would happen if the audiovisual system blew in the middle of the program. Think what would happen if you, the coordinator, got sick at the last minute. You can't plan for every eventuality, of course, but some things can be handled quickly if some forethought is given to them. It is the lack of forethought that often scuttles an otherwise good program when something goes wrong.

I was once asked to make a presentation to a professional group of educators about research on the faith development of adults. In those days, PowerPoint® had not appeared, so I prepared overhead slides to show the data. At the start of my presentation, I turned on the projector switch to show the first slide, and the bulb blew. My host had not thought about this possibility, so there was no backup bulb. Neither could he locate another projector in the hotel. Needless to say, my presentation, without the benefit of displaying the data, was a mind-numbing experience for the participants. Thinking defensively about what could possibly go wrong is an important component of effective program implementation.

8. Evaluate the degree to which the learning outcomes were achieved

Evaluation is a two-step process. The first step is to help learners diagnose how they did in the learning process. For example:

- Was it what they had expected?
- Did they achieve the learning outcomes or benefits as described? If not, what was the reason?
- What would have made the learning experience more beneficial?

- What more would they like to learn about this topic?

- Are there other topics that are important to them?

These are the kinds of questions that should be asked of learners as part of any evaluation process. The central focus is on helping them determine what they learned and how well they learned it. It is generally a good idea to keep the number of evaluation questions brief and to the point. Learners do not like long, drawn-out questionnaires, and the adult catechetical leader needs to know only what will help him or her do a better job next time.

Evaluations are most often done at the conclusion of a program or following each segment of a long program, such as a week-long seminar, but questionnaires can also be handed out and completed afterward. There are benefits to both methods. When evaluations are done immediately, each learner present at the program's end normally completes one. If the evaluations are handed out or posted online with a future completion date, a portion of learners may not get around to doing them. At the same time, some learners claim that they can give better feedback if they are given time to think more seriously about the questions.

Some learners are uncomfortable giving honest feedback unless they can do so anonymously. For this reason, adult catechetical leaders should ensure that completed forms are devoid of any identifying information, such as name, address, or occupation.

The adult faith formation committee does the second step of the evaluation. Like the learners, the committee is interested in knowing to what degree the learning outcomes were realized and how well the process worked. But the committee is looking at those questions as program providers, not as learners, and the findings of the two groups may differ.

How is that possible? Here is an example of how it can happen. The committee decides to invite a certain speaker and asks him to cover points a, b, and c. He is a gifted speaker, but time gets away from him and he covers only points a and b. Or, as happens all too frequently, the speaker starts with point a and then moves on to other points that are more to his liking. But because he is a gifted speaker, the learners give him high marks and are either unaware of the fact or simply forget that certain objectives were not met. The committee, however, is aware of the deficiency.

For many program providers, having a speaker who wows the participants, regardless of how sufficiently he or she addresses the topic, is what they care most about. If people go away happy, the committee is happy. And in most one-session programs, the failure of a speaker to cover all the points is not a major problem.

It can be a problem, however, if one set of outcomes depends upon the successful completion of earlier objectives. For example, suppose there is to be a multi-session program on the sacraments, and the leadoff speaker fails to lay the groundwork of sacramental theology that the remaining speakers are expected to build upon. If that speaker fails to do so, the committee has the problem of figuring out how to get the material covered so that the rest of the sessions can go as planned.

When used properly, evaluation is an important component of the entire planning process. It enables program providers to assess the effectiveness of their design and to make necessary adjustments to improve the quality of future learning sessions. Evaluation also serves as an important link to needs assessment by engaging learners in a thoughtful process of examining what more they would like to learn about the topic just covered or about other topics.

Converting one's vision for adult faith formation into reality is a matter of taking the time and care to plan and execute learning opportunities carefully. Whether one uses the major planning steps provided here or those in some other guide, it is essential that the planning process be taken seriously and be given the attention and effort it deserves. Catechetical leaders owe it to the adults they serve to ensure that the programs being offered are the result of careful attention to adult needs and due regard for them as mature and capable learners.

Questions for Reflection

1. Of the planning steps presented here, which one do you find most crucial to the success of the entire planning process?

2. What are the most difficult parts of the planning process for you to execute? What makes them so?

3. What are some of the more successful ways you have found to provide ongoing support to volunteers?

4. What do you find as the most reliable way of identifying the learning needs of parishioners?

5. Are there aspects of your parish life that give a different message than what you would like to present in an adult learning experience? If so, what are they?

6. What do you do to ensure that you have chosen the right design for your learning objective?

7. Besides what was mentioned in this chapter, what else can be done to help adult learners have a better sense of the organic integration of the Catholic faith?

Appendix

All materials in the Appendix can be downloaded free of charge at avemariapress.com.

Historic Milestones

The following events and documents played a significant role in development of adult faith formation over the past 80 years.

1926—The American Association for Adult Education (AAAE) is founded in order to gather and disseminate information concerning adult education aims and methods. Its research and publications gradually influenced thinking about approaches to adult religious education, especially in the 1960s and 1970s.

1943—*Divino Afflante Spiritu* is published. Encyclical of Pope Pius XII that promoted modern biblical studies. For the previous fifty years, the use of emerging methods of textual criticism was under a heavy cloud of suspicion, thereby curtailing scripture's emergence as a vital force in pastoral ministry, especially the ministry of the Word, where catechesis properly belongs.

1948—The Christian Family Movement (CFM) is founded. The movement was very popular in the years leading up to the Second Vatican Council and proved to be a highly successful approach to adult faith formation. Entirely lay-run, CFM produced an array of study materials based on the Jocist method of "Observe, Judge, Act," pioneered by Canon Joseph Cardijn, founder of the Young Christian Worker Movement in the 1920s. Other movements, such as Cursillo, Focolare, and Marriage Encounter, also began to play important roles in educating adults in the faith.

1954—*Triptych of the Kingdom: A Handbook of the Catholic Faith* by Van Doornik is published in Holland. This book laid the foundation for what later becomes *A New Catechism: Catholic*

Faith for Adults (1967), which had a major impact as a content resource in adult faith formation.

1962–1965—Second Vatican Council meets. The various decrees coming from the Council spark a strong interest in and a need for adult faith formation as changes in Church life begin to occur. Of particular importance was the decision in *Christus Dominus* (#44) to produce a directory for catechesis.

1968—The U.S. Bishops establish a Division for Adult Education at the U.S. Catholic Conference, which begins to produce *Focus*, a newsletter for adult education, and other publications.

1970—*The Modern Practice of Adult Education* by Malcolm Knowles is published. This book introduces the concept of "andragogy," the education of adults as contrasted with "pedagogy," the education of children. Andragogy becomes a major conceptual framework within religious adult education circles.

1971—*General Catechetical Directory* (*GCD*) is published in response to the directives of the Second Vatican Council. It establishes adult catechesis as the "chief form of catechesis" (#20).

1972—Latin version of *Rite of Christian Initiation of Adults* published, followed in 1974 by the English translation. The Rite has a profound impact on the formation process of all adults, not just catechumens.

1974—Third General Assembly of the Synod of Bishops addresses the topic of evangelization. The following year, the Apostolic Exhortation *Evangelii Nuntiandi* is published, which configures catechesis as a part of evangelization.

1978—Fourth General Assembly of the Synod of Bishop addresses the topic of catechesis. The following year, *Catechesi Tradendae* is published, which reiterates and expands on the centrality of adult catechesis. The document puts great emphasis on the need for a catechesis that is organic and systematic.

1979—*Sharing the Light of Faith: National Catechetical Directory for Catholics of the United States* is published. The directory is developed through a groundbreaking national consultation process, which utilizes adult learning principles.

1979—The National Advisory Committee on Adult Religious Education is established within the Department of Education, USCC. The committee produces a number of adult education resources and hosts a national symposium on adult faith formation in 1983. It later plays a major role in the development of both *Serving Life and Faith* and *Our Hearts Were Burning Within Us.*

1985—Extraordinary Assembly of the Synod of Bishops calls for "a catechism or compendium of all Catholic doctrine regarding both faith and morals" to be composed.

1986—*Serving Life and Faith: Adult Religious Education and the American Catholic Community* is published. This the first major national document on adult faith formation to be issued by the USCC, with the approval of the Committee on Education.

1988—The International Forum on Adult Religious Education meets for the first time in London, England, through an initiative of the adult religious education personnel of the Bishops' Conference of England and Wales. The forum, which meets every two years, is a network of adult religious education personnel and members of national advisory committees. Meetings have been held in locations ranging from Europe and North America to India, Thailand, and Chile.

1990—International Council for Catechesis publishes *Adult Catechesis in the Christian Community.* The document offers guidelines for effective adult catechesis, with particular emphasis on the Christian community's dependence upon systematic adult catechesis.

1994—*Catechism of the Catholic Church* is published and becomes the chief content resource for bishops, catechetical leaders, and publishers.

1997—*General Directory for Catechesis* (*GDC*) is published. The new general directory considerably expands the 1971 version. It highlights enculturation as a major issue, and reemphasizes catechesis as a moment within evangelization and adult catechesis as a top priority. It also underscores the RCIA as the model for all catechesis.

1999—*Our Hearts Were Burning Within Us* is published. This is the U.S. Bishops' pastoral plan for adult faith formation in the United States. It lays out both principles of good adult faith formation as well as suggested steps for parishes and dioceses to put the plan into action.

2005—*National Directory of Catechesis* is published. This document is a U.S. adaptation of the *General Directory for Catechesis*. As such, it includes sections on the catechetical implications of United States. society and the organization of pastoral ministry in accordance with the structures and systems of the Catholic Church in the United States. It also reiterates the long-held directive that adult catechesis is the Church's chief form of catechesis.

2006—*United States Catholic Catechism for Adults* is published. Provides an adaptation of the *Catechism of the Catholic Church* for both Latin and Eastern Catholics living in the United States. Unlike the *CCC*, which was addressed to bishops and catechetical leaders, the *USCCA* is intended for general adult use.

Relevant Ecclesial Documents Concerning Adult Faith Formation

Paul VI, Apostolic Exhortation *Evangelli Nuntiandi*, December 8, 1975

This was a breakthrough document in many ways. It asserts that the Church exists to evangelize. It places catechesis within the overall movement of evangelization and acknowledges that the proclamation of the Gospel is done primarily by witness. It also encourages adapting evangelization to the language, signs, and symbols of people's lives. The key section on catechesis is found in #44:

> A means of evangelization that must not be neglected is that of catechetical instruction. The intelligence, especially that of children and young people, needs to learn through systematic religious instruction the fundamental teachings, the living content of the truth which God has wished to convey to us and which the Church has sought to express in an ever richer fashion during the course of her long history. No one will deny that this instruction must be given to form patterns of Christian living and not to remain only notional. Truly the effort for evangelization will profit greatly—at the level of catechetical instruction given at church, in the schools, where this is possible, and in every case in Christian homes—if those giving catechetical instruction have suitable texts, updated with wisdom and competence, under the authority of the bishops. The methods must be adapted to the age, culture and aptitude of the persons concerned, they must seek always to fix in the memory, intelligence and heart the essential truths that must impregnate all of life. It is necessary above all to prepare good instructors—parochial catechists, teachers, parents—who

are desirous of perfecting themselves in this superior art, which is indispensable and requires religious instruction. Moreover, without neglecting in any way the training of children, one sees that present conditions render ever more urgent catechetical instruction, under the form of the catechumenate, for innumerable young people and adults who, touched by grace, discover little by little the face of Christ and feel the need of giving themselves to Him.

John Paul II Apostolic Exhortation
Catechesi Tradendae (CT), October 16, 1979

This document came out of the Fourth General Assembly of the Synod of Bishops, which had been presided over by Paul VI the previous year. Two important sections excerpted here are the pope's emphasis on the need for an organic and systematic catechesis (#21) and the section specifically related to adult faith formation (#43).

> **21.** In his closing speech at the fourth general assembly of the synod, Pope Paul VI rejoiced "to see how everyone drew attention to the absolute need for systematic catechesis, precisely because it is this reflective study of the Christian mystery that fundamentally distinguishes catechesis from all other ways of presenting the word of God."

In view of practical difficulties, attention must be drawn to some of the characteristics of this instruction:

- It must be systematic, not improvised but pro-grammed to reach a precise goal;

- It must deal with essentials, without any claim to tackle all disputed questions or to transform itself into theological research or scientific exegesis;

- It must nevertheless be sufficiently complete, not stopping short at the initial proclamation of the Christian mystery such as we have in the kerygma;

- It must be an integral Christian initiation, open to all the other factors of Christian life.

I am not forgetting the interest of the many different occasions for catechesis connected with personal, family, social and ecclesial life—these occasions must be utilized—but I am stressing the need for organic and systematic Christian instruction, because of the tendency in various quarters to minimize its importance.

43. To continue the series of receivers of catechesis, I cannot fail to emphasize now one of the most constant concerns of the synod fathers, a concern imposed with vigor and urgency by present experiences throughout the world: I am referring to the central problem of the catechesis of adults. This is the principal form of catechesis, because it is addressed to persons who have the greatest responsibilities and the capacity to live the Christian message in its fully developed form. The Christian community cannot carry out a permanent catechesis without the direct and skilled participation of adults, whether as receivers or as promoters of catechetical activity. The world, in which the young are called to live and to give witness to the faith which catechesis seeks to deepen and strengthen, is governed by adults. The faith of these adults too should continually be enlightened, stimulated and renewed, so that it may pervade the temporal realities in their charge. Thus, for catechesis to be effective, it must be permanent, and it would be quite useless if it stopped short at the threshold of maturity, since catechesis, admittedly under another form, proves no less necessary for adults.

International Commission on English in the Liturgy

Rite of Christian Initiation of Adults, July 1, 1988.

The RCIA has been cited in other major documents, e.g., *General Directory for Catechesis* (*GDC*) #90, as the model for all catechesis. Number 75 spells out the essential formation process that serves as the "model" for catechesis.

> The Catechumenate is an extended period during which the candidates are given suitable pastoral formation and guidance, aimed at training them in the Christian life.[1] In this way, the dispositions manifested at their acceptance into the Catechumenate are brought to maturity. This is achieved in four ways:
>
> 1. A suitable catechesis is provided by priests or deacons, or by catechists and others of the faithful, planned to be gradual and complete in its coverage, accommodated to the liturgical years, and solidly supported by celebrations of the word. This catechesis leads the catechumens not only to an appropriate acquaintance with dogmas and precepts but also to a profound sense of the mystery of salvation in which they desire to participate.
>
> 2. As they become familiar with the Christian way of life and are helped by the example and support of sponsors, godparents, and the entire Christian community, the catechumens learn to turn more readily to God in prayer, to bear witness to the faith, in all things to keep their hopes set on Christ, to follow supernatural inspiration in their deeds, and to practice love of neighbor, even at the cost of self-renunciation. Thus formed, "the newly converted set out on a spiritual journey. Already sharing through faith in the mystery of Christ's death and resurrection, they pass from the old to a new nature

made perfect in Christ. Since this transition brings with it a progressive change of outlook and conduct, it should become manifest by means of its social consequences and it should develop gradually during the period of the Catechumenate. Since the Lord in whom they believe is a sign of contradiction, the newly converted often experience divisions and separations, but they also taste the joy that God gives without measure."[2]

3. The Church, like a mother, helps the catechumens on their journey by means of suitable liturgical rites, which purify the catechumens little by little and strengthen them with God's blessing. Celebrations of the word of God are arranged for their benefit, and at Mass they may also take part with the faithful in the liturgy of the word, thus better preparing themselves for their eventual participation in the liturgy of the eucharist. Ordinarily, however, when they are present in the assembly of the faithful, they should be kindly dismissed before the liturgy of the eucharist begins (unless their dismissal would present practical or pastoral problems). For they must await their baptism, which will join them to God's priestly people and empower them to participate in Christ's new worship (see no. 67 for formularies of dismissal).

4. Since the Church's life is apostolic, catechumens should also learn how to work actively with others to spread the Gospel and build up the Church by witness of their lives and by professing their faith.

---

1. See Vatican Council II, *Decree on the Church's Missionary Activity, Ad Gentes,* #14.
2. Ibid., no. 13.

International Council for Catechesis

Adult Catechesis in the Christian Community: Some Principles and Guidelines, 1990

Although this document does not carry the same level of authority as either an apostolic exhortation or general directory, it nonetheless offers important guidance from the Vatican on adult faith formation. The following sections are especially notable.

> **21**. Adults in the Church, that is, all Christian men and women, lay people, priests, and religious are people who have a right and an obligation to be catechized just like everyone else (*CT*, c. V; can. 217, 774; *Christifideles Laici* (Chr. L.) 34).
>
> This reason does not derive from any kind of service which the adult Christian is called to render. It springs instead directly from the "seed" of faith planted within and which hopes to mature as the adult grows in age and responsibility. "When I was a child I used to talk like a child, think like a child, reason like a child. When I became a man I put childish ways aside" (1 Cor 13: 11).
>
> Only by becoming an adult in the faith is one able to fulfill his or her adult duties toward others, as is required by the vocation given to each at baptism.
>
> One must admit that in various communities, the formation of adults has been taken for granted or perhaps carried out in connection with certain events, not infrequently in an infantile way. Because certain external or traditional supports are sometimes lacking, a grave imbalance is created insofar as catechesis has devoted considerable attention to children while the same has not happened in the catechesis of young people and adults.

22. The need for personal formation is necessarily bound up with the role which adults assume in public life. They share with all Christians the task of witnessing to the Gospel in words and deeds, but they do this with undeniable authority and in a specifically adult way. This is true in the family context in which many adults, precisely as parents or other relatives, become both by nature and grace the first and indispensable catechists of their children. Adults also serve as role models for young people who need to be confronted with and challenged by the faith of adults.

In the context of society, the role of adults is crucial in the workplace and in the academic, professional, civil, economic, political and cultural spheres, and wherever responsibility and power are exercised. This is the case because the believing adult is so often the only one who can introduce the leaven of the Kingdom, express the novelty and beauty of the Gospel, and demonstrate the will for change and liberation desired by Jesus Christ.

The simple, faith-filled actions by which adults give witness to the Gospel in these situations require a great effort on their part to inwardly appropriate what they are called to pass on to others in a convincing and credible way.

25. In summary, in order for the Good News of the Kingdom to penetrate all the various layers of the human family, it is crucial that every Christian play an active part in the coming of the Kingdom. The work of each will be coordinated with and complementary to the contribution of everyone else, according to the different degrees of responsibility each one has. All of this naturally requires adults to play a primary role. Hence, it is not only legitimate, but necessary, to acknowledge that a fully Christian community can exist only when a systematic catechesis of all its members takes place and when an effective and well-developed catechesis of adults is regarded as the central task in the catechetical enterprise.

69. Adult catechesis necessarily aims at making the adult a member of and a participant in the community. This means that adults must not only know the community, but must also actively participate in its various faith expressions and accept some form of responsibility for community life. For this reason, the building of small communities or ecclesial groups is conducive to the strengthening of adult catechesis (cf. *CT* 24).

Congregation for the Clergy

General Directory for Catechesis, 1997

The *GDC* provides a substantial number of directives on the catechesis of adults. And given the amount of material it devotes to the topic, it is difficult to adequately represent here the key points. Still, paragraph 175 stands out for its description of the major tasks of adult faith formation.

175. So as to respond to the more profound needs of our time, adult catechesis must systematically propose the Christian faith in its entirety and in its authenticity, in accordance with the Church's understanding. It must give priority to the proclamation of salvation, drawing attention to the many difficulties, doubts, misunderstandings, prejudices and objections of today. It must introduce adults to a faith-filled reading of Sacred Scripture and the practice of prayer. A fundamental service to adult catechesis is given by the *Catechism of the Catholic Church* and by those adult catechisms based on it by the particular Churches. In particular, the tasks of adult catechesis are:

– *to promote formation and development of life in the Risen Christ* by adequate means: pedagogy of the sacraments, retreats, spiritual direction . . . ;

– *to educate toward a correct evaluation of the socio-cultural changes of our societies in the light of faith*: thus the Christian community is assisted in discerning true values in our civilization, as well as its dangers, and in adopting appropriate attitudes;

– *to clarify current religious and moral questions,* that is, those questions which are encountered by the men and women of our time: for example, public and private morality with regard to social questions and the education of future generations;

– *to clarify the relationship between temporal actions and ecclesial action,* by demonstrating mutual distinctions and implications and thus due interaction; to this end, the social doctrine of the Church is an integral part of adult catechesis;

– *to develop the rational foundations of the faith*: that the right understanding of the faith and of the truths to be believed are in conformity with the demands of reason and the Gospel is always relevant; it is therefore necessary to promote effectively the pastoral aim of Christian thought and culture: this helps to overcome certain forms of fundamentalism as well as subjective and arbitrary interpretations;

– *to encourage adults to assume responsibility for the Church's mission and to be able to give Christian witness in society:* The adult is assisted to discover, evaluate and activate what he [or she] has received by nature and grace, both in the Christian community and by living in human society; in this way, he [or she] will be able to overcome the dangers of standardization and of anonymity which are particularly dominant in some societies of today and which lead to loss of identity and lack of appreciation for the resources and qualities of the individual.

United States Conference of Catholic Bishops (USCCB)

Our Hearts Were Burning Within Us: A Pastoral Plan for Adult Faith Formation in the United States, 1999

This bishops' statement presents an overview of the ministry of adult faith formation and identifies specific action steps to make it a top priority in parishes throughout the country. Excerpted here are several paragraphs on the priority of adult faith formation.

> 39. We are convinced that the energy and resources we devote to adult faith formation will strengthen and invigorate all the charisms that adults receive and the activities they undertake, in the Church and in society, to serve the Gospel of Christ and the people of today. Every Church ministry will be energized through a dynamic ministry of adult catechesis.

> 40. Adult faith formation also benefits children and youth. An adult community whose faith is well-formed and lively will more effectively pass that faith on to the next generation. Moreover, the witness of adults actively continuing their own formation shows children and youth that growth in faith is lifelong and does not end upon reaching adulthood.[14]

> 41. In addition, adult faith formation should serve as the point of reference for catechesis for other age

groups. It ought to be "the organizing principle, which gives coherence to the various catechetical programs offered by a particular Church."[15] Maturity of faith is the intent of all catechesis from the earliest years. Thus, all catechesis is geared to a lifelong deepening of faith in Christ. How necessary, then, that the catechetical ministry with adults set an example of the highest quality and vitality.

14. *Catechesi Tradendae*, no. 43.
15. *GDC*, nos. 59, 171, 275.

United States Conference of Catholic Bishops

National Directory for Catechesis, 2005

The *NDC* is the latest authoritative statement from the U.S. bishops on the ministry of catechesis. Excerpted here are the recommended methodological principles for adult faith formation (NDC 48.A).

Several principles should guide the selection of effective methods for adult catechesis:

- Since adults "have a right and a duty to bring to maturity the seed of faith sown in them by God,"[610] they should identify their catechetical needs and, with the help of those responsible for religious education, plan ways to meet those needs.

- Those responsible for adult catechesis should identify the principal characteristics of adult Catholics, develop catechetical objectives based on those characteristics, and design a catechetical plan to meet those objectives.

- Those responsible for adult catechesis should determine the most effective methods and choose formats and models that represent a "variety of forms: systematic and occasional, individual and community, organized and spontaneous."[611]

- Those responsible for catechesis should identify the members of the community who can serve as catechists for adults and should provide for their training, formation, and spiritual enrichment.

- Adult catechesis should respect the experiences of adults and make use of their personal experiences, skills, and talents.

- Adult catechesis should be based on the circumstances of those to whom it is addressed: their situations as adults; their racial, cultural, religious, social, and economic conditions; their experiences and problems; and their educational and spiritual maturity.

- Adult catechesis should recognize the specific conditions of lay Catholics and consistently call them to holiness and to "seek[ing] the Kingdom of God by engaging in temporal affairs and ordering them according to the plan of God."[612]

- Adult catechesis should involve the whole community so that it may be a welcoming and supportive environment.

- Adult catechesis requires a comprehensive, multifaceted, and coordinated approach and a variety of learning activities, such as participation in liturgical experiences, Scripture reading and study, retreats and experiences of prayer, family or home-centered activities, ecumenical dialogues, small-group experiences, large-group experiences, and individual activities.[613]

- As much as possible, adult catechesis should involve adults themselves in the catechetical process so that they can teach and learn from one another.

---

610. *GDC*, no. 173.
611. *General Catechetical Directory*, no. 19.
612. *Christifideles Laici*, no. 9.
613. Cf. *Our Hearts Were Burning Within Us*, nos. 100–112.

The Parish as a Teaching Community

Everything the parish does and how it does it teaches something about the Catholic way of life. The following list is a guide for evaluating what the parish is communicating about Catholic life through its activities and its structures.

What Do We See Our Parish Communicating about Catholic Life in the Way We:

1. celebrate our liturgies and common prayer life?

2. promote and offer catechesis for all ages?

3. evangelize within and beyond the parish?

4. reach out to our youth and young adults?

5. include and learn from our minority populations?

6. serve and utilize the gifts and skills of people with disabilities?

7. support families as domestic churches?

8. promote and engage in works of justice and charity?

9. welcome and incorporate new members into the community?

10. foster a sense of belonging and mutual care as a community?

11. focus on mission in terms of looking beyond our own needs and interests?

12. allocate our funds in support of our mission?

13. exercise our leadership roles?

14. empower members for service?

15. utilize the gifts, skills, and resources of the community?

16. use our facilities to support our needs, our mission, and our strategic goals?

17. create and maintain a warm and friendly environment throughout our facilities?

18. utilize our communication channels, e.g., bulletin, website, e-mail?

19. provide just wages and benefits to our employees?

20. collaborate with other parishes, Christian denominations, and faith communities?

21. allocate our personal and communal resources for good stewardship?

22. other?

Sample Letter of Appointment to the Adult Faith Formation Committee

Date

Inside address

Dear _____,

It has come to my attention that you have agreed to serve on our Adult Faith Formation Committee. I am delighted with this news and wish to extend to you my heartfelt gratitude and deep appreciation for the work you have agreed to undertake. Adult Faith Formation is at the center of the Church's catechetical ministry, and as you know, we at _____ (name of parish) take the faith formation of our adult members very seriously. So it is especially pleasing to me that you will be bringing your gifts and talents to this very important work.

Should you have any questions along the way or wish to meet with me about your ministry, please don't hesitate to contact me. I will be keeping you and the other adult faith formation committee members in my prayers.

Sincerely yours in Christ,

Pastor or Parish Administrator

Program Planning Guide
and Checklist

This worksheet is only a guide and should be adapted for the particular circumstances of the program and the parish. Due dates and persons responsible for specific functions should be identified next to each item.

Program:

1. Title:

2. Goal:

3. Objectives:

4. Date and time:

5. Location:

Resources:

1. Speaker / Facilitator:
   - Name:
   - Written agreement (spelling his / her duties):
   - Honorarium / stipend:
   - Transportation arrangements:
   - Lodging:
2. Books:
3. Handouts:
4. PowerPoint®:
5. Online course / resources:

Equipment:

1. Computer/overhead projector:
2. LCD projector:
3. Tape recorder:
4. CD player:
5. Easel or chalk board:
6. Electrical cords, surge protectors:
7. Audio (microphones and speakers):
8. Backup equipment, e.g., extra bulbs:

Hospitality:

1. Registration:
2. Signage (directions to event, restrooms, etc.):
3. Name tags, handouts:
4. Refreshments/meals:
5. Childcare:
6. Transportation for elderly, people with disabilities:
7. Wheelchair access:
8. Cleanup:

Facilities:

1. Setup for seating and table arrangements, etc.:
2. Lighting, audio, and temperature control:
3. General environment (decorations, plants, indirect lighting, etc.):

4. Setup for prayer, liturgy, music ministry:

5. Tear down/clean up:

Program Implementation:

1. Program moderator:
   - Welcome, introductions:
   - Overall facilitation:
   - Evaluation process:
2. Group facilitators:
3. Liturgy/prayer (musicians/singers, celebrant):
4. Pencils, paper:
5. Evaluation forms:

Promotion/Publicity:

1. Campaign schedule:
2. Campaign methods (flyers, bulletin, e-mail, website, personal contact, direct mail, etc.):

Contingency Plans:

1. Loss of speaker:
2. Equipment breakdown:

Committee Evaluation:

1. Attainment of objectives:
2. Planning process:
3. Resources (speaker, other):
4. Budget/finances:

Program Budget:

1. Income:
   - Registrations fees: _____
   - Other income: _____
   - Total: _____
2. Expenses:
   - Speaker/Facilitator: _____
   - Audiovisual rentals: _____
   - Printed materials: _____
   - Program materials: _____
   - Refreshments/food: _____
   - Environment: _____
   - Musicians: _____
   - Equipment: _____
   - Publicity: _____

- Childcare: _____
- Transportation: _____
- Miscellaneous: _____
- Total: _____

Intergenerational Catechesis: Considerations and Resources

In recent years, intergenerational or "whole community" catechesis has gained popularity with a growing number of parishes and some dioceses in the United States. Advocates and practitioners of this approach to catechesis see it as an improvement over traditional forms of catechesis for children and a boost to adult faith formation.

In 2006–2007, the Bishops' Committee on Catechesis, to which I was a consultant, explored the nature and implications of intergenerational catechesis. While the committee recognized the renewed fervor in catechesis often displayed by parishes using an intergenerational approach, they also voiced some cautions about it. First, they wanted to ensure that recent gains in catechesis resulting from the publication of major catechetical documents, such as the *Catechism of the Catholic Church* and the general and national catechetical directories, not be compromised. For example, they felt that through the use of the "protocol" based upon the *CCC*, significant improvements had been made in the catechetical texts that serve as a bedrock of traditional catechetical programs. They did not want to see intergenerational catechesis abandon these important catechetical resources in favor of yet unproven approaches.

Second, they also wanted to ensure that all forms of catechesis, including intergenerational catechesis, are systematic and comprehensive. They wanted curricula in place that developed along with children as they grew in age and maturity. For these and other reasons, they thought it best that intergenerational catechesis be more of an adjunct to traditional catechesis than a replacement for it.

To date, no national study on intergenerational catechesis has been done to provide data on its overall effectiveness, especially as contrasted with traditional catechesis. Still, practitioners have voiced some common observations from their experience. What follows is a very limited list of "hints from the field" for those considering or having embarked on intergenerational catechesis. The above concerns of the Committee on Catechesis should also be kept in mind.

Adult Faith Formation

- Most adult participants find intergenerational learning a non-threatening way to explore their faith with others.

- Some adults are stimulated by the intergenerational experience to want to learn more about their faith. Parishes can and should offer additional learning opportunities to meet this need.

- Intergenerational learning, by definition, is not a comprehensive adult faith formation program. Adults need separate learning opportunities that are geared to their level of experience and state in life.

- Parents need to be trained and given adequate tools to be the primary educators of their children. This is even more crucial than in traditional catechesis.

Program Development

- Pastors, parish administrators, and other parish leaders should be encouraged to speak confidently and enthusiastically about the new catechetical paradigm if it is to succeed.

- Pastoral leaders and staff need to be sensitive to and supportive of the collaboration that must take place across ministry boundaries.

- Demands on staff may increase given the challenges of coordination and other logistical issues and must be planned for accordingly.

- Given the significant liturgical underpinning of whole community catechesis, there needs to be a strong emphasis on liturgical catechesis and the utmost care given to the celebration of the liturgy.

- There should be opportunities for parish leaders involved in the program to share ideas for continued improvement.

- There should be opportunities for families that have enjoyed the program to give testimony about its benefits to fellow parishioners.

- Good resources should be made available for at-home learning activities.

- As with all catechetical formats, intergenerational catechesis needs to be firmly grounded in the principles of the *GDC* and *NDC*.

- Intergenerational learning often works best when blended with a traditional catechetical format.

Resources to help:

- www.lifelongfaith.com. This is the website for **LifelongFaith Associates**. Its major projects and programs include publishing a quarterly journal, *Lifelong Faith*, and sponsoring the "Faith Formation in Christian Practices Project" with resources for households and churches.

- www.pastoralplanning.com. This website was founded by Bill Huebsch, author of

Whole Community Catechesis. It offers multiple resources to support lifelong faith formation in parishes. It also offers services in leadership development, parish staff development and sacramental formation.

- Bill Huebsch, *Whole Community Catechesis* (New London, CT: Twenty-Third Publications, 2005).

- Bill Huebsch, *Dreams and Visions: Pastoral Planning for Lifelong Faith Formation* (New London, CT: Twenty-Third Publications, 2007).

- Bill Huebsch, *A Pastor's Guide to Whole Community Catechesis* (New London, CT: Twenty-Third Publications, 2004).

- Kathy Hendricks, *The How-To's of Intergenerational Catechesis* (National Conference for Catechetical Leadership, 2005).

- Mariette Martineau, Joan Weber, and Leif Kerwald, *Intergenerational Faith Formation: All Ages Learning Together* (New London, CT: Twenty-Third/Bayard Publications, 2007).

Designing Promotional Material

Promotional material is the "face" of your program. It should exhibit a thoughtfulness and professionalism that project the quality of the program itself.

Ten commandments for quality and effectiveness in promotional material:

1. Keep it *concise*. Use short paragraphs and short, direct sentences.

2. Keep it *readable*. Use adequate size headlines and font sizes. Use good paper to ink contrast. Make your copy stand out.

3. Keep it *neat*. Watch for ink bleed-through, crooked copy, and smudges.

4. Keep it *spacious*. Use lots of "white" space, generous margins. Don't have the copy look constricted.

5. Keep it *scanable*. Employ frequent use of headlines, art, and separate blocks of copy. Short lines preceded by bullets (dots) work well.

6. Keep it *active*. Use strong, active verbs. Avoid the passive voice. Place the most important items up front. Make sure your program's outcomes and benefits stand out.

7. Keep it *personal*. Use first- and second-person pronouns. Use names. Build in personal quotes, testimonials.

8. Keep it *durable*. Use adequate weight paper to better withstand the rigors of mailing and to feel more professional in the hands.

9. Keep it *economical*. Use computer-based design templates and paper with pre-existing color graphic designs to avoid design and printer costs.

10. Keep it *timely*. Get your material out with enough lead-time for busy people to be able to schedule in the program.

Approaches to Learning Needs Analysis

Determining the learning needs and interests of parishioners is a complex matter that benefits from a variety of approaches. Below are listed a number of ways to secure information about learner needs and interests, categorized according to "less formal" and "more formal."

Less Formal

- Observation—Attending to what parishioners talk about and express interest in or concern about. Paying attention to what they read/borrow from the parish library or buy from the bookrack. This also includes observing what programs draw interest in neighboring parishes.

- Media—Doing a regular analysis of what the media is covering in magazines, news reports, and TV features. What's in the news is generally what is on people's minds.

- Suggestion box—Encouraging parishioners to drop in their topics of interest in suggestion boxes strategically located throughout the parish.

- Leadership interviews—Interviewing the pastor and other key parish leaders who work directly with parishioners about their impressions of parishioners' learning needs and interests.

- Pastoral visits—Using an existing pastoral visitation program to inquire about learning interests.

- Liturgical year—Drawing on the heightened interest in spiritual issues that usually accompany liturgical seasons, such as Lent and Advent.

More Formal

- Small groups—Convening groups of parishioners who volunteer to meet to discuss potential adult faith formation program offerings. These can be done at after-Mass coffee klatches, when parents drop children off for religious education, or at other available times when people gather.

- Post-learning-session evaluations—Using the evaluation process of a program to inquire about what else the learners are interested in.

- Questionnaire—Sending out, e-mailing, or posting on the parish's website a well-designed questionnaire for parishioners to complete. Questionnaires can also be sent home with the children in religious education or at the parish school. However, direct mail to a randomly selected group is most effective for securing valid information.

- Telephone interview—Calling randomly selected parishioners with several well-formulated questions about learning interests. The callers are trained to conduct the interview in the same way to ensure valid data collection.

Adult Faith Formation
and the Liturgy

The Rite of Christian Initiation for Adults has heightened awareness of the intrinsic link between adult faith formation and the liturgy. In paragraph 75, we read that the catechesis of candidates should be "accommodated to the liturgical year, and solidly supported by celebrations of the word."

Both the *General Directory for Catechesis* and the *National Directory for Catechesis* call for the RCIA to serve as the "model" or "inspiration" for all catechesis. For this reason, the North American Forum on the Catechumenate and the National Conference on Catechetical Leadership hosted a national symposium earlier this decade to explore ways in which the RCIA could serve as the inspiration for catechetical ministry. Insights from the symposium are presented in *An Apprenticeship in the Christian Life: Exploring the Baptismal Catechumenate as Inspiration for All Catechesis* by Marie Kordes and Loyes Spayd. The book is available from both organizations at www.naforum.org and www.nccl.org.

Many adult faith formation leaders have sought to base some or all of their programs on the liturgical year. Publishers and organizations have responded to this need by creating a variety of resources.

The Archdiocese of Detroit offers an extensive online list of liturgically based adult learning resources that are available from a wide range of publishers. To access the list, go to www.aodonline.org. Click on Offices and Ministries, then Education, then Adult Faith Formation, then Programming Resources, then Lectionary-Based Adult Scripture Study.

Some catechetical leaders have found *Ministry and Liturgy Magazine* helpful in their efforts to connect adult faith formation with the liturgy. It can be accessed at: http://www.rpinet.com/ml.

Two organizations that have made consistent efforts to provide assistance in resources and consulting for the liturgical dimensions of adult faith formation are LifelongFaith Associates at www.lifelongfaith.com and Pastoral Planning at www.pastoralplanning.com.

1. Vincent J. Miller, *Consuming Religion* (New York: Continuum, 2005), 224.
2. *General Catechetical Directory* (1971) #20. While this document is no longer in print, it can be accessed online at www.vatican.va. (See also *NCD*, # 188, *CT* #43, *GDC*, #59, *OHWB* #13, *NDC* p. 187.)
3. Matthew 28:19.
4. Apostolic Exhortation *Evangelii Nuntiandi* (1975) #14. This document can also be accessed at www.vatican.va.
5. *National Directory for Catechesis* (Washington, D.C.: United States Conference of Catholic Bishops, 2005), 188–190.
6. *Evangelii Nuntiandi, #*14.
7. 1 Peter 3:15.
8. Bishop Blasé Cupich, "Handing on the Faith through Community-Based Faith Formation: Our Common Challenge and Shared Privilege," in *Handing on the Faith: The Church's Mission and Challenge* (New York: The Crossroad Publishing Company, 2006).
9. See the pastoral letter at: http://www.rcbo.org/learning-loving-living-faith/letter-on-faith.html#read.
10. *Evangelii Nuntiandi* #73.
11. *Adult Catechesis in the Christian Community: Some Principles and Guidelines* (International Council for Catechesis, Libreria Editrice Vaticana, St. Paul Publications, 1990), #25. This document can be found at www.vatican.va.
12. Ephesians 4:15.
13. 1 Corinthians 2:16.
14. See the complete research report online at http://pewresearch.org/pubs/743/united-states-religion.
15. "Willow Creek's 'Huge Shift,'" *Christianity Today* (June 2008), 13.
16. William V. D'Antonio, "Generational Differences: Survey of U.S. Catholics," *National Catholic Reporter* (September

30, 2005). The article is part of a national survey report. The survey results and accompanying commentary by the researchers can be accessed online at www.ncronline.org. The survey appears in book form in William D'Antonio, James Davidson, Dean Hoge, and Mary Gautier, *American Catholics Today: New Realities of their Faith and their Church* (Lanham, MD: Rowman and Littlefield, 2007).

17. Clifford Geertz, *Islam Observed* (Chicago: University of Chicago Press, 1971), 17.
18. James D. Davidson, "Challenging Assumptions about Young Catholics: Survey of U.S. Catholics," *National Catholic Reporter* (September 30, 2005).
19. Thomas P. Rausch, *Being Catholic in a Culture of Choice* (Collegeville, MN: Liturgical Press, 2006), 5.
20. Michele Dillon and Paul Wink, *In the Course of a Lifetime: Tracing Religious Belief, Practice, and Change* (Berkeley: University of California Press, 2007), 211.
21. Robert Wuthnow, *After the Baby Boomers: How Twenty- and Thirty-Somethings Are Shaping the Future of American Religion* (Princeton, NJ: Princeton University Press, 2007), 133.
22. John M. Hull, *What Prevents Christian Adults From Learning?* (Philadelphia: Trinity Press International, 1991), 208.
23. John 1:46; Matthew 16:15.
24. John Paul II, "Letter founding the Pontifical Council for Culture," May 20, 1982.
25. Michael Paul Gallagher, S.J., *Clashing Symbols: An Introduction to Faith and Culture* (New York: Paulist Press 1998), 115.
26. As quoted in Idries Shah, *Learning How to Learn: Psychology and Spirituality in the Sufi Way* (San Francisco: Harper & Row, 1981), 141.
27. Gallagher, 116.
28. Ibid., 114.
29. Matthew 13:1–9.
30. *GDC*, 158.
31. *Origins* 14, no. 36 (Feb. 21, 1985), 601.

32. Robert Duggan, *Best Practices for Parishes*, at www. bestpracticesforparishes.org. The reader may see preview copies of the program, in particular the best practice statements for catechesis.
33. Kenneth Stokes, *Faith Is a Verb: Dynamics of Adult Faith Development* (Mystic, CT: Twenty-Third Publications, 1989), 71.
34. Robert N. Bellah, Richard Madsen, William M. Sullivan, Ann Swidler, and Steven M. Tipton, *Habits of the Heart: Individualism and Commitment in American Life* (New York: Harper & Row, 1985), 226.
35. Hans Küng, *The Church* (New York: Sheed and Ward, 1967), 86.
36. Wuthnow, 223.
37. Jacqueline L. Salmon, "Big Church Not Always Impersonal, Study Finds," *Washington Post* (Sept. 19, 2008), A6.
38. Wuthnow, 51.
39. International Council for Catechesis, *Adult Catechesis in the Christian Community (ACCC)*, at www.vatican.va, #28.
40. Bellah, 239.
41. See Appendix entry on intergenerational learning.
42. Wuthnow, 230.
43. James T. Burtchaell, *Philemon's Problem: The Daily Dilemma of the Christian* (Chicago: ACTA, 1973), 140–141.
44. Augustine, *Sermons*, 272.
45. Michael J. Himes, "Communicating the Faith: Conversations and Observations," in *Handing on the Faith*, edited by Robert P. Imbelli (New York: The Crossroad Publishing Company, 2006), 121–122.
46. For an overview of the research into neuroplasticity see Sharon Begley, *Train Your Mind: Change Your Brain* (New York: Ballantine Books, 2007).
47. Malcolm Knowles, *The Modern Practice of Adult Education* (New York: Association Press, 1970), 51.

48. As quoted in Robert M. Smith, *Learning How to Learn: Applied Theory for Adults* (Chicago: Follett Publishing Company, 1982), 60.

49. Knowles, 39–44.

50. Gordon W. Allport, *The Individual and His Religion* (New York: Macmillan Publishing, 1950), 60.

51. Smith, 43.

52. Howard Gardner, *Multiple Intelligences: New Horizons in Theory and Practice* (New York: Basic Books, 2006).

53. Augustine, *The Teacher*, 11:38, 14:45.

54. Richard A. McCormick, S.J., "The Shape of Moral Evasion in Catholicism," *America* 159, no. 8 (October 1, 1988), 188.

55. As quoted in Pico Iyer, "The Eloquent Sounds of Silence," *Time*, January 25, 1993.

56. Ibid.

57. Rowan Williams *Where God Happens: Discovering Christ in One Another* (Boston: New Seeds, 2005), 43.

58. Anne Morrow Lindberg, *Gift From the Sea* (New York: Vintage Books, 1955), 84–88.

59. Augustine, *The Trinity*, 4:4.

60. As cited in Gabriel Moran, *Fashioning a People Today: The Educational Insights of Maria Harris* (New London, CT: Twenty-Third Publications, 2007), 115.

61. *GDC*, 139.

62. Rainer Maria Rilke, "Letter 4: July 16, 1903," in *Letters to a Young Poet*. There are multiple Web sites that have the ten letters that comprise this collection.

63. Thich Nhat Hanh, *The Miracle of Mindfulness* (Boston: Beacon Press, 1987).

64. Eudora Welty, *One Writer's Beginnings* (New York: Warner Books, 1984), 16.

65. Private e-mail.

66. Bellah, 221.

67. Christelyn D. Kerazin, "Digital Learners: The Morphing of Education," in *Vistas* 11, no. 2 (Summer 2008), 26.

68. The parish website can be accessed at: www.transfiguration.com.
69. Go to: http://speakingoffaith.publicradio.org.
70. Go to: www.nationalcathedral.org.
71. The *Catechism of the Catholic Church* can be found in its entirety online at www.vatican.va.
72. See www.rcl.web.com.
73. ACCC, #59.

Neil Parent served as Executive Director of the National Conference for Catechetical Leadership from 1990 to 2007. Prior to this position, he served for twelve years as Representative for Adult Education at the United States Conference of Catholic Bishops. In this capacity, Parent edited ten books on adult catechesis, all published by the USCCB. He has written numerous articles for such publications as *Our Sunday Visitor*, *Catechetical Leader*, and *Faith Alive*. Additionally, Parent served seven years as Director of Adult Faith Formation at Blessed Sacrament Parish in Alexandria, Virginia. He now teaches and works as an independent consultant for Catholic organizations, parishes, and dioceses.

Founded in 1865, Ave Maria Press,
a ministry of the Congregation of
Holy Cross, is a Catholic publishing
company that serves the spiritual and
formative needs of the Church and its
schools, institutions, and ministers;
Christian individuals and families; and
others seeking spiritual nourishment.

For a complete listing of titles from

Ave Maria Press

Sorin Books

Forest of Peace

Christian Classics

visit www.avemariapress.com

ave maria press / Notre Dame, IN 46556
A Ministry of the Indiana Province of Holy Cross